# BEAVER BEHAVIOR
## Architect of Fame & Bane!

by Morrell Allred

Naturegraph

**Library of Congress Cataloging in Publication Data**
Allred, Morrell, 1917—
    Beaver Behavior.

    1. Beavers.   I. Title.
QL737.R632A45      1986          599.32'32
ISBN 0-87961-154-5
ISBN 0-87961-155-3 (pbk.)

*Beaver illustration on title page and 108 is by Byron Alexander. All other photos and illustrations, except as noted in captions, are from the author, Morrell Allred.*

*Naturegraph* Publishers, Inc.
P.O. Box 1075
Happy Camp, California 96039
U.S.A.

# CONTENTS

A beaver lodge in a cove on the beautiful Yellowstone River.

## Chapter One

# KING OF THE BEASTS

Who would believe that a small animal could start a world war? Or impel the exploration and conquest of a continent? Yes, there is just such an animal—the beaver.

*What is a beaver?* Known the world over as an ambitious "chap," the beaver carries a wide variety of connotations depending upon one's particular experience—or lack of it—with our buck-toothed friend. Almost everyone seems to pass judgment upon him; he is either famous or infamous, depending on one's esteem for "unlaziness." Witness the cliches "eager beaver" and "busy as a beaver."

Students of nature see the beaver as a most wonderfully adapted and intelligent creature—one of the very few capable of modifying its environment while creating habitat for many other kinds of animals as well as for plants. Do I remember the two-foot-wide stream we called Second Creek! It babbled its musical but uneventful way off Big Ridge in two forks which met a mile above its junction with Spring Creek. It was uneventful until the summer a pair of beavers built a dam just below its forks. The next spring I heard mallards conversing contentedly on the pond. Frogs came, too. The ducks nested nearby and in midsummer a "train" of yellow-brown ducklings followed their mother triumphantly across the pond. A muskrat waggled his tail while hunting food among the new sedges. That summer the beavers built two more dams a short distance downstream and erected a small lodge beside the main pond. They were rather retiring, so I saw neither them nor the secret number of cub beavers they raised. No matter. Second Creek had come to life. It would not be the same again.

The fisherman's esteem for the beaver is often quite emphatically either pro or con. The critter either created or ruined his favorite fishing hole. In either case it created a home for too many mosquitoes. But the day-loving fisherman rarely sees a beaver. My wife was an exception. She had a favorite fishing hole on the stream not far from our house. While there one evening about sunset she had an unexpected visitor—a big, fat beaver. She froze very still, lest any movement or sound might frighten him. After swimming a few trips across the fishing hole the animal went on about its business. Each time my wife went there to fish in the evening that summer, Mr. Beaver arrived, too, as if by prior appointment. He gained so much confidence that

The beaver. Photo from *The Plain Truth* magazine.

one night he decided to become still better acquainted; he came ashore and straight up the bank toward her, while wriggling his nose the better to smell all about his new friend. She became quite nervous, of course, facing those big buck teeth at five feet. That was as close as he wanted to be. He abruptly returned to the water, diving with a big splash and a loud slap of his tail upon the water.

The fur trapper views the beaver as a most intelligent and wary animal—an exciting challenge to his ingenuity and a rewarding prize when he masters the techniques of beaver capture. To some men the lure of beaver trapping borders on addiction. The fur trade—the recipients of the product of the trapper—does not think of the beaver as an animal at all. To these folks "beaver" is a round, flat piece of merchandise (perhaps a reminder of the good old silver dollar). When made into garments the merchandise is the most durable fur known. The fur from damaged beaver skins and the fur by-products from coat manufacture make the finest quality felt.

To the fashion world beaver is a beautiful and durable fur garment. When sheared, let down and fashioned into a coat, beaver skins bear little resemblance indeed to the little creature from whence they came. A look at the price tag might cause one to believe that all people in the beaver business are very rich. Not so; there is much labor and expense between the beaver and the proud owner of a beaver coat.

Students of history recognize that the beaver was a motivating influence in the exploration and conquest of the North American continent. I was awed as I stood on the "roof" of the continent at South Pass, in Wyoming. This is a comparatively low, smooth break in the rugged mountain range which divides the waters of the Atlantic and Pacific oceans. From here endless desolation reigns formidably in all directions. To the west it is some 40 miles (60 kilometers) to sufficient water for even a drink, not to even mention enough water for harboring beavers. Nevertheless, the South Pass was discovered by who else but beaver trappers! In a successful bid to "save their hair" (escape scalping by Indians), they fled far southward from their intended route over the mountains as they returned eastward toward home. They crossed the divide at this low place, not knowing what an important route they had found. Not many years later wagons crossed the mountains there and the Old Oregon Trail came into being.

Some Indian tribes delved somewhat deeper into what a beaver might be (though some of us might not understand their methods). The Crows believed in the reincarnation of man into the form of a beaver. Therefore, the beaver deserved special respect, for any beaver could be a deceased relative or friend. The Cherokees believed it was the beaver which created the continents by dredging them up from the primeval seas. Thus they recognized the beaver as a great engineer. People of our day also increasingly recognize the engineering expertise of the beaver. Those familiar with his works see him as an engineer whose structures man cannot duplicate.

Taxonomists (biologists who classify living creatures) have named the European beaver *Castor fiber* and the North American beaver *Castor canadensis*. The beaver is a mammal (Class *Mammalia*) and the largest of rodents (Order *Rodentia*). The beaver is from the Family *Castoridae* (animals having glands which manufacture, store, and discharge castorium), and form the Genus *Castor*, and the two general species *fiber* and *canadensis*. There are 24 subspecies (varieties within a species) in the range of *C. canadensis*, which includes most of North America north of Mexico.

After having lived next door to Mr. Beaver for well over half a century, I have perhaps become a bit more biased in his favor than other men—excluding, perhaps, our Indian friends. And we must remember that such is not the unanimous sentiment among human neighbors. Well, this neighbor has earned my respect as an engineer, as well as for how "smart" he can be upon occasion. In other words, he has made a bumbling fool of me time and again. For example, on one of the many occasions when I was requested to remove the beavers from an irrigation canal across which they were building dams and depriving the farmers' crops of needed water, I set traps, but when I returned to pick up the beavers, I found only sprung traps. The traps had been visited and put out of commission without catching beavers. This continued each morning for a week. I became desperate—I just *couldn't* admit to those farmers that I could not catch a beaver! One evening, determined to find out what was happening, I went to "stake" them out at about 30 yards downwind from a trap. All was quiet until dark. Then a big beaver approached the trap, and I thought surely I would be privileged to witness a catch at last, though by then visibility was dim. But no! He just turned about and slapped his tail up and down on the water straight above the trap until the agitation sprung the trap!

Well, I learned some tricks, too, and was able to catch enough beavers so that I can say that Mr. Beaver has paid my taxes and lifted my mortgages. More importantly, however, he has drawn me into the bosom of nature, into the pitifully small remnant of frontier America, over trails traveled by Indians, mountain men and pioneers. Oft'times I wondered, did Indians camp here? which of the mountain men came this way? or, who built this trail? In these places, midst grandeur and solitude, I pondered the beaver's works and his ways.

Not only have I dwelt with him in my day, but through some study of history have learned that the beaver's earlier impact upon the affairs of men is immeasurable—unbelieveable! So far as I can discover, no other undomesticated animal has even begun to exert such an effect upon the course of human history.

Of greater moment now, however, is the beaver's relationship to mankind as a fellow citizen in our world community of life. Assuming that aesthetic values are a mere luxury (which I do not), and from a purely practical point of view, the beaver is a dominant figure in our world of nature—a superb ecologist and conservationist as well as a renewable resource. His full potential value is neither recognized nor appreciated by mankind in general.

Therefore, not because of his terrifying roar (he's not a "big-mouth") nor his physical prowess (he's no bully), but as a consequence of his past, present, and future importance to the fortunes of mankind, I proclaim our modest and humble-appearing buck-toothed friend, the beaver, to be *The King of the Beasts!*

And, forthwith, I'll prove it.

## Chapter Two

## THE BEAVER IN MAN'S PAST

Would it be an exaggeration to claim that the Oregon Trail was built by Mr. Beaver? The trails across Canada? Except for the beaver, when would the first flags have been unfurled over western North America? Or might they have been the flags of Spain, Russia, or China, rather than those of Canada and the United States? How could the intermountain west have been settled without the discovery of South Pass and the subsequent Oregon Trail across the Rocky Mountains?

The beaver's influence upon the course of western history is indeed unique in the animal kingdom. ". . . So important was the pursuit of the beaver as an influence in westward movement of the American frontier that it is sometimes suggested that this fur bearer would be a more appropriate symbol of the United States than the bald eagle."(Enc. Am. 12:178, 1969). Canada's late historian, Harold Innis, recognized the beaver as the central figure in the exploration and conquest of the North American continent.

### The Quest for the Treasure

The quest for the treasured beaver is a most fascinating drama of human history. It began in the royal courts of Europe, where the top hat became the symbol of distinction. These top hats were made of felt, and felt is made of wool or fur, and the finest felt is made of beaver fur. Presumably to protect his consumer subjects from the fraud of cheap substitutes, King Charles I, of England, is purported to have decreed in 1638 that, "Nothing but beaver stuff or beaver wool shall be used in the making of hats." Like all status symbols, the article was sought also by the lesser nobility, resulting in the higher nobility having their hats made even higher, thus preserving their distinction. Hence the expression "high hat" to denote aristocracy and arrogance. The higher the hat the more felt was required and the more devastation inflicted upon the beavers. The supply of European beavers was soon exhausted and the species suffered near-extinction. Beaver advocates then turned to the New World with its "inexhaustible" supply. It was there that our great beaver panorama unfolded.

Who of us can begin to imagine the feeling within the beaver-clad breast of the New World native on the North Atlantic coast when he first beheld a great, tall ship from Europe sailing in majesty to his shore? We may be quite certain, however, that he had no idea of the treasures it carried—treasures he could possess for merely swapping his old, worn-out beaver coat. Innis reprints a historic account stating that on their first encounter with a French trading ship one entire group of Indians, ". . . bartered all they had to such an extent that all went back naked without anything on them; and they made signs to us that they would return on the morrow with more furs . . ." We may raise eyebrows at the European preference for the Indian's old beaver coat. Innis explains:

". . . The pelts were taken by the Indians when prime and the inner side scraped and rubbed with the marrow of certain animals. After this treatment each pelt was trimmed into rectangular shapes and from five to eight were sewn together with moose sinews into robes which were worn by the Indians with the fur next to the body. The scraping of the inner side of the pelt loosened the deep roots of the long guard hair, and with wearing, this hair dropped out leaving the fur. With constant wearing for fifteen to eighteen months the skins became well greased, pliable, and yellow in colour and the fur downy or *cotonné*. These furs taken in winter when prime were known later as *castor gras d'hiver.* It was this fur which was most valuable to the hatmaking industry. The guard hairs had largely disappeared and the fur was especially suited to the felting process."

It would be difficult to say which was the more thrilled with what the other had to trade, the Indians or the Europeans. We, of such an affluent age, are not prepared to comprehend what the sudden emergence from the stone to the iron age meant to the Indian. From the accounts we have it would be difficult to overstate the impact of iron on the Indian economy at the beginning of their beaver trade with the French. Of all the wonders wrought in iron which the whites brought, kettles were the most valuable to the natives. They were portable, thus freeing the villagers to travel far from the huge stone kettles which they heretofore used. Closely following the kettle in value were knives, awls, axes and, of course, firearms. These trade goods were well chosen by the French, for not only were they of great value to the natives, but all items made possible a greater harvest in beaver.

Small wonder, then, that the Indians regarded the first traders with the awe befitting deity. Innis quotes some of the early explorers and traders, ". . . the savages showed a marvellously great pleasure in possessing and obtaining these iron wares and other commodities, dancing and going through many ceremonies. . . . we gave them knives, glass beads, combs and trinkets of small value, at which they showed many signs of joy, lifting their hands to heaven and singing and dancing in their canoes . . ." And, "The Hurons think that the greatest rulers of France are endowed with the greatest powers, and having such powers can make such things as hatchets, knives, kettles . . ."

All the Indian needed to attain the iron age and the good life were beavers. And about all the white traders wanted were beavers. Many beavers. The Indian had them; and they cost him nothing. Innis reports one Indian saying in banter, ". . . In truth, my brother, the beaver does everything to perfection. He makes for us our kettles, axes, swords, knives and gives us drink and food without the trouble of cultivating the ground . . ." And Hiram Chittenden, author of *American Fur Trade in the Far West* (1935), wrote, "The white man valued the native furs altogether beyond what the Indian was able to comprehend, and the latter was only too happy to find that he could trade them for that gaudy and glittering wealth which had been brought from a great distance to his country. Thus, in the early intercourse of the white man with the Indian, each gave to the other something he valued lightly, and received in return something that he valued highly, and each felt a keen contempt for the stupid taste of the other."

Before the white man arrived the Indian satisfied his need for beavers by lying beside the animal's lodge at sunset with arrow fitted to bow while waiting for the triangle shaped top of the beaver's head to emerge on the pond. Following the swish of the arrow there may have been a triumphant yell followed by a great splash as the hunter plunged into the pond to retrieve his prize before it sank to the bottom. Otherwise, life was calm. Beavers were plentiful; the need for beaver and methods for aquiring them were in balance.

With the coming of the white trader, demand for beaver suddenly outstripped the renewable supply. Innovative natives responded to the demand with the organized beaver hunt. A team of hunters built a stake corral surrounding the beaver's lodge to prevent any from escaping, then unceremoniously pulled the lodge apart and used their dogs to locate the prey in adjacent tunnels and bank dens. (One can almost still hear the excited barking of dogs mingled with the yelling and laughing of men.) This was mass production. It produced beavers by the colony in a single hunt—and more of the bounties from across the seas. That the resource base was being destroyed must be ignored, because if this group of hunters didn't do it a competing tribe or white hunters would. Thus, a centuries-old intertribal agreement forbidding such waste of natural resources was repudiated. But times were changing. The demand for beavers—ever more and more beavers—was stronger than reason.

Why worry? There were plenty of beavers inland—beavers without number. Both hunters and traders pushed inland like a plague, crossing forbidden tribal boundaries where necessary; violating hunting agreements when necessary. Word went forth via middlemen traders, both white and red, to tribes still farther inland to hunt beavers and reap the rich rewards the white men brought. The results were more and more beavers for a time, but also more and more troubles.

The waterways were the avenues of commerce. Convoys of birch canoes heavily laden with precious beaver skins enroute to trading posts became common. Husky, near-naked oarsmen at bow and stern plied both lakes and streams. Pirates, unprincipled rivals and those seeking redress for trespass by the hunters, lurked about along bank and shore, seeking opportunity for plunder or revenge.

The Iroquois Indians held the land in the lower St. Lawrence River area. During the early days of the beaver trade, commerce of other tribes had to cross their lands and waterways to reach the trading posts. An armed conflict between the Iroquois and the more western and northern tribes ensued for many years. In the meantime the Dutch settled at the mouth of the Hudson River and became competitors to the French. They traded firearms to the Iroquois—something the French had been careful not to do. It was said that, hazardous as were the river rapids to the bark canoe convoys, the oarsmen dreaded the Iroquois more. Ironically, much as the Iroquois disrupted the flow of beaver skins to their trading posts, the French did not want peace between the Indian tribes for fear that the Iroquois would then lead the other tribes to deliver their beavers to the Dutch.

While venturing farther inland, the beaver hunters and middlemen traders also fanned to the northwest and southwest. Between waterways, backbreaking overland portages of furs, trading goods and canoes were made on hazardous trails. Such names as Grand Portage and Portage La Prairie still bear witness of the way-stations built at portage terminals. This system extended the reach into beaver sancturaries far into the Northwest.

The portage problem was eased greatly in many places by an ingenious someone with a sharp axe, a handsaw and a steel auger bit. He fashioned from bits of forest about him two wheels that were both light and strong, and stood taller than a big man. He added a hardwood axle, a basketlike willow box and a pair of shafts. The high wheels rode the mud holes, spanned the chuck holes and could be pulled over small logs with relative ease. It could be pulled by men—or squaws—but the luxury of having an ox was preferred. Despite the screeching and screaming from friction between axle and hub, the "Red River Cart" provided overland transportation, and well served its purpose of bringing more beavers to market.

Farther to the south and west, men strove against swift river currents, deserts and mountains as they expanded to the interior beaver streams and lakes. Horses were eventually employed in beaver trade. The steel trap was invented to increase the take of beaver. Now the beavers could be captured while the trapper slept. The steam engine and its application to special-built boats relieved backbreaking upstream travel on large rivers, still furthering the demise of the beaver. The Indian was caught in a dilemma. As the beavers on his own tribal lands disappeared, he must either move westward into hostile territory in search of more of them, or be left without medium of exchange. Articles which were once luxuries became necessities; he could no more do without an iron knife or kettle than you or I could live without electricity, automobiles or telephones.

## The French Founded the American Fur Trade

The North American Fur Trade was founded by the French government. Their traders began dealing with the Indians along the North Atlantic coast during the 16th century. Their competition with the Dutch and the English was to come later. The fur trade, principally beaver, was at first incidental to the fishing trade, but it grew rapidly and spread inland. In about 1625, the Caen brothers were reported to have traded for 22,000 beaver skins.

The first important French trading post was built at Montreal, where an annual fur fair was held. Some later French trading centers, were at Mackinac Island in the strait between Lakes Huron and Michigan, at Detroit and at Green Bay. From its point of beginning near Montreal, the trading area of the Europeans spread to the northwest, west and southwest like a great fan until it spanned the continent.

The policy of the French government was to maintain a strict monopoly over the fur trade. All men were expected to work under the direction of the government-chartered fur company. Some men, however, went looking for beavers and failed to return to civilization. Apparently word came back that they had not perished, for others soon followed their example. The taste of freedom, adventure—and perhaps new romance—was stronger than country ties. These beaver hunters lived with the Indians as free men. The government reacted by declaring them outlaws. Thus did the beaver cause men to become outlaws to their government. The loyal French referred to them as *coureurs de bois* (bush-rangers or woods runners). These men and their halfbreed offspring traveled deep into the interior of the continent in search of beavers. The French names they gave to some of these places remain to this day as testimony of their penetration. At about the time of the loss of New France to England, it was estimated that perhaps 800 men—half of the male population of the colony— were living as outlaw *coureurs de bois*. It is interesting to note that by exploring and establishing fur trading posts in the Great Lakes region and along the Mississippi River, France had succeeded in cutting off England's westward expansion in the New World. Ironically, it was the outlawed beaver hunters who opened the way for their government's expansion and advantage over the English competition.

As displaced Indians, and adventurous French, English and Dutch pressed inland looking for more beavers, treaties were broken; friends became bitter enemies. Too numerous to mention separately were the military engagements and small incidents between English and French, Indians and both English and French, and intertribal strife among the Indians in connection with the beaver trade. Innis' account is replete with mention of them, but no details are given.

Then who caused the French and Indian War, as the Americans named it? Why, the beaver, of course. The history books tell us it was French and English rivalry in the New World. So it was—rivalry over the beaver trade. Incidentally, this war— known in Europe as the "Seven Years War"—developed into somewhat of a world conflict. But who would accuse a mere beaver of inciting a world war? At the conclusion of the war, England was the possessor of New France and all of the French trading posts. France had dominated the New World beaver trade for about 200 years. The onslaught upon the beaver continued unabated under British control.

## The British Fur Trade Monopoly

Who caused the Canadians to remain British at the time of the American Revolution? Again, it appears definitely to have been the beaver. Following their acquisition of the French holdings, the British, through their giant Hudson's Bay Company (founded in 1670), enjoyed a fur trade monopoly in the New World for a few decades. The sweet taste of monopoly might be exemplified by the reported exchange rate in trade based upon blanket sized (see page 108 for pelt sizing) beaver: A large beaver bought 1/10 of a gun; 1/2 pound of gun powder; 2 pounds of shot; 1/2 pound beads; one hatchet; or 1/12 of a wool blanket. In the northern, nonagricultural regions of the continent, all of the people—both Indian and white—became dependent upon Hudson's Bay Company for their supplies—and beaver was the medium of exchange. Thus, the government-chartered trading company pretty well ruled the destinies of those engaged in hunting or trapping animals of any kind.

The American Revolution is reported to have had no immediate effect upon the British fur trade. Interestingly, it has been said that the Canadians remained loyal to the crown because they literally had a beaver economy. They were dependent upon the Hudson's Bay Company, which in turn was dependent upon the crown and upon Parliament. Thus, it appears that it was the beaver which caused Canada to remain British.

As might be expected, the challenge to the Hudson's Bay Company's fur trade monopoly came from the Americans once they were free, and it grew in rapid intensity considering the meager resources and small population of the new republic. President Thomas Jefferson read about Britain's Alexander McKenzie discovering in 1789 a great beaver-bearing river flowing to the Arctic (which was to bear his name); and of McKenzie reaching the Pacific Ocean in 1793 via the Continental Divide while searching for a short route to the Chinese fur market. Jefferson could scarcely have realized the great worth of the continent. The vast wilderness west of the Mississippi was unknown, but it was quite certain to harbor a great treasure of beaver. This large western half of the continent would be claimed by England if America did not act quickly. (Of course Jefferson could visualize much more than mere fur trade wealth for his young country; he sought a greatly expanded, strong republic, with secure boundaries where his political ideals could be nourished and bear fruit.) The fur resources would provide both the incentive and pay for the movement.

## America Enters the Fur Trade

The Louisiana Purchase of 1803 acquired for the United States the entire western half of the Mississippi Valley and extended in length from the Gulf of Mexico to Montana, thus doubling the land area of the nation. During the same year, Lewis and Clark proceeded toward the mouth of the Missouri River, carefully selecting and recruiting their expeditionary force as they went. Both the Louisiana Purchase and the 1804 - 1806 Lewis and Clark expedition opened the vast wilderness west of the Mississippi to the people of the United States for fur trade, and for any other use they might find for it.

With the Louisiana Purchase, the United States acquired St. Louis, the newly-established French fur trade headquarters of the West. It was originally built by them just before the French and Indian War as one of their chain of trading centers in the interior. Strategically located near where the Mississippi and the Missouri rivers meet, it became not only the fur trade center of the United States, but also headquarters for the westward movement of the nation.

In 1805, Lewis and Clark crossed the continental divide and pushed on to the Pacific Ocean, spending the winter of 1805 - 1806 near the mouth of the Columbia River. On their return trip in 1806, when they reached the Mandan Indian villages on the banks of the Missouri where North Dakota would one day be, one of their men, John Colter, caught the "trapping fever," secured his release from their service and went back up the river with two companions looking for beaver. The next year he conducted Manuel Lisa, a trapper-trader of Spanish descent to the mouth of the Bighorn River (now in Montana) to establish a fur trading post deep in the wilderness. Lisa held a trapping and trading franchise from the French government extending over the Osage Indian territory (probably the largest exclusive beaver trapping area on record).

While with Lisa, Colter was sent alone on a mission to the

Crow Indians to solicit their beaver skins. He again crossed the continental divide with them and into a valley (Pierre's Hole, and later renamed Teton Valley, in eastern Idaho), where he was wounded in a battle between his hosts and the Blackfoot Indians. He was probably the first white man to see this rich beaver producing area. As he returned alone through the mountains toward the Missouri, he discovered the phenomena of the future Yellowstone Park.

In 1808, John Jacob Astor founded the New York fur trade and two years later sent a ship around Cape Horn to establish the Pacific Fur Company at the mouth of the Columbia River, thus giving American claim to the beaver-rich Pacific Northwest. In 1809, David Thompson of the Northwest Fur Company—an organization of British free traders in competition with the Hudson's Bay Company, as well as with the onrushing Americans—entered future United States territory on the Pacific slope to build a trading post near where the town of Hope, Idaho, would be. In the meantime, a group of St. Louis traders formed the American Fur Company, established trading posts along the Missouri River, and in 1810, sent Andrew Henry with a party of trappers westward across the continental divide in search of more beavers. Finding it necessary to spend the winter west of the divide, Henry and his men built Fort Henry near the future site of St. Anthony, Idaho.

Also in 1810, Astor sent Wilson Price Hunt with a party of 65 men across the continent to explore suitable sites for fur trading posts in the interior and to make contact with the party at the mouth of the Columbia. They reached Fort Henry via Pierre's Hole in October of 1811. But in attempting to navigate the treacherous Snake River, their boats capsized, they lost all their equipment and almost perished before reaching the Columbia.

## Exploitation of the Beaver in the Northwest

The British seized Astor's Pacific Fort and Trading Post during the War of 1812, thus temporarily thwarting the United States' claim to the Columbia Basin.

In 1813, the Pacific Fur Company's Reed party established trapping headquarters on the Boise River in an attempt to claim the Columbia Basin. They were killed by Indians a few months later.

The Northwest Fur Company and the Hudson Bay Company, their British rivals, merged in 1821 as the Hudson's Bay Company in a concerted effort to compete with the Americans for both territory and beavers. The Americans rose to the challenge. After establishing posts along the Missouri River, they swarmed across the mountains to challenge the rights of the Hudson's Bay Company to the Columbia River drainage. The disputed area was known as the Oregon Territory, but it included all of present Oregon, Washington and Idaho, as well as parts of other states and southern British Columbia. It remained in contest until the treaty of 1846, at which time the compromise boundary along the forty-ninth parallel was established. During the many years of contest, both parties concentrated their efforts upon taking as many beavers as possible from the contested area to prevent their rivals from acquiring them.

General William H. Ashley and Andrew Henry organized the Rocky Mountain Fur Company at St. Louis in 1822. By 1823 their trappers reached the Snake River portion of the Columbia Basin. Chittenden tells us that Ashley took 100 packs of beaver from the Rocky Mountain area in 1824, 123 packs in 1826, and 130 packs in 1827. He estimated that in five years Ashley accumulated 500 packs for a total of 40,000 beavers with a value of $250,000, a great fortune in those days. He then sold his company to some of his men and retired.

Peter Skene Ogden, of the Hudson's Bay Company, entered the Snake River territory via Lemhi Pass in the spring of 1825 after traveling through the mountains most of the winter. In his *Ogden's Snake Country Journals*, he told how he hurried in an attempt to beat the Americans to the beavers in the Snake Indian country that spring—and every day thereafter until he returned to Canada in July of 1826. He trapped the year around, as did the "Mountain Men" of the United States. When a woman of his party gave birth to a child—and this happened several times during the expedition—he permitted the camp to remain for one day. His trappers did not celebrate the birth through rest, however; they were busy. His account tells how many beavers they took each day. He also tells us that he met General Ashley in the mountains and alleges that the American cheated him out of most of his beaver furs and lured away most of his men. (From other accounts, it appears that Ogden was short of whiskey, but Ashley was not.)

It was the year 1832 when man's activities converged upon the last of the beaver's vast domain. Captain Bonneville, on leave from the United States Army, took the first wagon over South Pass to the Green River in the future Wyoming. (He spent about three years in the Rockies trapping and perhaps gathering military information on the activities of the British.) It was the year that Nathaniel Wyeth, an eastern merchant, went west with the hope of making a fortune in furs and fish. It was the year in which the first steamboat—built specially for the purpose—ascended the Missouri River to serve the trading posts there. This awed the Indians to the extent that they ceased trading with the Hudson's Bay Company in that area, and took their trade to the Americans on the Missouri, giving the American Fur Company a strong advantage. Nevertheless, this same year some of the American Fur Company beaver trappers crossed the mountains and began very active and unethical competition to the Rocky Mountain Fur Company.

Thus it would appear that by 1832 the Rocky Mountain region—the last of the New World to be exploited of beaver—was teeming with trappers. The Pierre's Hole rendezvous and the battle of Pierre's Hole with the Blackfoot Indians took place this same year. It was estimated that 1,000 people assembled for this event.

The rendezvous was an innovation of Ashley's in 1824. It was simply a meeting in the mountains of traders and trappers. It might be called a portable trading post. No doubt it gave Ashley a competitive edge over his rivals, for by 1832 the American Fur Company joined in by self-invitation. This added to the spirit, color and competitive aura of the occasion. The meet lasted for several weeks, or until the trading was completed and the liquor all consumed.

What a sight this motley group must have been! If there were assembled a thousand people, how many were women and children (or were they even counted)? How many of each race? How many mixed breeds? How many horses were there? Sublette, who was in charge of the Rocky Mountain Fur Company's supplies, arrived from the East with 60 men and 180 pack horses—a total of 240 horses in that string. The American Fur Company's pack string was likely comparable. The trappers and Indians also had many horses.

When the parties finally dispersed, each went its own secret (if they could keep it) way. The Rocky Mountain Company headed for Teton Pass enroute to St. Louis with 168 packs of furs—eighty-four pack horses with a pack of furs on each side. Each pack contained some 80 beaver pelts and weighed about 100 pounds. Thus the Rocky Mountain Company acquired about 13,000 beavers and some miscellaneous furs. Though I have found no figure, it should be safe to assume that the American Fur Company acquired its share. The Hudson's Bay Company was also an active competitor in the area though it did not participate in the rendezvous.

Though the mountain area was the last to be exploited of it's beavers, and was the scene of intense competition, some areas to the north were managed better and continued in more stable yield. The total beaver exports from North American to Europe in the early nineteenth century have been estimated at 200,000 per year.

## The Wiles of the Frontier

Chittenden estimated that in twelve years the Rocky Mountain Fur Company acquired 1,000 packs of beaver worth $500,000. The company lost 100 men (killed) and had a property loss of $100,000.

Of the 200 men employed by Wyeth—a man from the East who attempted to enter the fur trading business—only forty remained alive after three years.

The early frontier was wild, raw and unforgiving. The beaver hunters were mostly very young, adventurous and inexperienced. These factors combined to make very high mortality statistics. Some examples: A small group of Rocky Mountain Fur Co. men were ambushed by Indians near the Teton Pass. One of Wyeth's trappers went to set traps along a small stream and did not return. His companions spent a few hours the next day looking for him, then went on. A teenaged boy in Wyeth's employ refused to embark into the "bull boat" and lead his horse behind while crossing the Snake River during high spring runoff (snow melt).

He insisted on riding his horse across. Both rider and horse disappeared into the raging, muddy current and were not seen again.

Chittenden noted the wages of the men and the prices they paid to the companies for a few necessities: The average wages of company men engaged in western fur trade between 1815 and 1830 were $150 per year. Beaver traps cost $9 to $12 each; soap $1.25 per pound; sugar $1 per pound; coffee $1.25 per pound; raisins $1.50 per pound; gun powder $1.50 per pound; scarlet cloth $6 per yard; horse shoes and nails $2 per pound; handkerchiefs $1.50 each; fourth proof rum, reduced $13.50 per gallon.

The price of beaver in the mountains during this period was from $2 to $4 per pound, or an average of near $3 per skin.* These prices, of course, affected only the free white trappers and the Indians, who were not on company salary. From these data one would be forced to conclude that the only costs in line with wages were those of death and burial.

Chittenden wrote that by 1842 there were six competing fur companies in the Rocky Mountains. Their trappers traveled and worked in various sized detachments for mutual protection. We may presume that though they may not have explored very systematically, this was compensated for by dedication to purpose. It appears that they located and trapped out every stream, lake and pond in the region, decimating the beaver population like a plague.

By 1843, the first wagon train of settlers crossed the mountains on the Oregon Trail. Most mountain men retired or sought employment as guides. And no wonder! The exploitation and decimation of beaver, buffalo and Indian was quite complete. Mountain man and free-roaming Indian faded into history. But what about the beaver?

---

* The felt trade, being interested only in the volume of fur (wool to them), bought beaver by the pound in about three different grades. In the early years of the trade, the worn Indian beaver coat from which the coarse guard hairs had fallen was top grade, the prime heavily-furred pelt second, and the thinly-furred summer pelt was lowest grade. Since it was not feasible for traders to weigh small quantities, it became a practice on the frontier to trade on a per skin basis with a grading system based on size as well as fur density.

## The Plight of the Beaver at the End of an Era

Yes, what about the beaver? After all, the beaver was the prey—the hunted—the object of it all. In other words, it was he who caused all of this ruckus. The beaver provided for the red man's entrance to the iron age—and provided for his destruction by luring the white man in to despoil his land and destroy his economy. The beaver had been the object of a concentrated onslaught for almost 300 years! How could it possibly survive its hunters?

But the beaver survived them all—though barely. It had disappeared from most of its range in Europe, east of the Mississippi in the United States, and was very scarce in the Rocky Mountains and Western Canada.

Now who would believe that the beaver was saved from extinction by a worm? Such may very well have been the case, for top hat fashion turned to silk, and beaver, after hundreds of years of front-page prominence, was out of favor. The economic depression of the early 1840's, combined with the already depressed beaver market and extreme shortage of beaver in the wilds, precipitated the end to an era. By 1843 the era of the beaver trade with the Indian and the fur-company-sponsored white trappers in United States territory lapsed into history.

Both mountain men and Indians were permanently out of the fur business, the beaver practically out of existence. By then every nook and corner of the West was familiar to the mountain men. A wagon road was made across the plains and mountains and on to the Pacific following generally the trails discovered by beaver hunters. Many of the trappers therefore became guides to the onrush of settlers. The impetus for the movement was provided by the near-extinct and almost-forgotten beaver.

In Canada, where the trade was under government control and such wholesale exploitation was prevented, the Hudson's Bay Company has continued its operations, with some adaptive modifications. It was reported to have traded for more than three million beaver pelts between 1853 and 1877.

## The Comeback of the Beaver

The survival of the beaver in United States territory was precarious for the balance of the nineteenth and early twentieth centuries. Though its fur was not sought with the intensity of former years, it was still of some commercial value. The removal of the Indians to reservations gave the beaver little respite, for the Indians were replaced by settlers.

Relief to the beaver came slowly as, one by one, the states passed protective laws and reintroduced the animals into regions where they had been extirpated. It wasn't until 1936, however, when beaver skin traffic was placed under federal control, that the beaver's population recovery became fully secure, for poached (illegally taken) skins had been of such magnitude as to keep beaver numbers low. The federal requirement of an official metal tag on each skin, a strict inspection and report policy, and high penalties for infractions, terminated poaching.

When fully protected, the beaver's increase was so spectacular that by 1940 some states began harvesting them as surplus in selected areas. The renewed demand for beaver, developing just a century after its decline from favor, was not for felt hats, but for women's fur coats. A new manufacturing process in which the outer fur was sheared rather than plucked (as had been done), was developed. It left a plush velvetlike material with the back-to-belly fur color blending from near black to pearl gray. The product was very rich-looking, durable and desirable, and once again "beaver" became a household word.

Beaver pelt prices soared—reaching perhaps as much as $100 per pelt for the very top grades. State coffers enlarged. State trappers prospered and landowners with beaver habitat enjoyed a "slice of the pie."

At the same time, beaver conservation was *in,* and the valuable resource was nurtured. Long dried-up ponds became wet and alive again from beaver immigration and transfers by man. In many places, the mallard, after a hundred years of silence, quacked happily once more. Moose stood knee-deep in satisfaction. Trout were introduced into many a new beaver-made pond. Biological communities became more diverse. Some landowners decided their land was more valuable for beaver culture than for agriculture. Attempts were made to pen-raise mutant-colored beavers, but with limited early success.

Then quite as suddenly as it began, the "honeymoon" of beaver and man ended. Beaver was suddenly shunned by fickle Dame Fashion in favor of the elegant ranched mink available in a variety of attractive mutant colors. The beaver market became burdened with oversupply.

During the 1950's, our short-lived hero gradually became the derelict. No longer was he welcome to plug irrigation ditches and highway culverts, and to fell shade and fruit trees. His caved-in bank dens became deadfalls to cussing fishermen and ranchers. Some grazing associations demanded his removal from their forest grazing allotments on the grounds that he was flooding too much forage and too many access roads.

As this situation developed, state agencies stopped trans-planting beavers and began extensive trapping and skinning; but skins were so cheap they wouldn't pay the cost of trapping. And what does one do with a damage-claim beaver which must be removed in summertime when his pelt is worthless, but there is no place he is welcome alive? While arriving at solutions to these problems, trapping was delayed in some areas so long that the overpopulated beavers depleted their food supply.

In some states, the problem was at last bestowed upon private trappers who operated under state supervision. Very liberal quotas were allowed the trappers, who were willing to perform cheap labor as a reward for being permitted to trap beavers. From the states' standpoint, the fewer beavers the less headache for the game and fish department—a policy which was probably justifiable for the short term.

## The Beaver's Future

The beaver's past has been most exciting and important to man—and most precarious to the beaver. His future is in the hands of state conservation agencies. Their methods of regulation vary with many local conditions—ecological and political. The beaver's future will thus depend upon man's estimate of his value as a natural resource, of his ecological potential, and his value as a fellow creature.

## Chapter Three

## ADAPTATIONS WHICH MADE A BEAVER

Would you believe there is an animal with one foot adapted to work in solid materials and another foot adapted to work in liquid? Yes, the beaver is built that way! He is most wonderfully adapted in many ways to his environment and habits of life. That is, he has specialized equipment which he uses expertly to accomplish the purposes for which the equipment was designed. All creatures in nature—both plants and animals—have their exclusive adaptations, in both form and function. In other words, animals have special tools which they know how to use. Using them is behavior, or function.

Most biologists accept the premise that the vast differences, or variety, among the creatures we see in nature resulted from each kind gradually acquiring differing adaptive organs over many generations of time, which equip them for their many differing ways of life. The behavior to properly use this equipment is acquired simultaneously. For examples: wings developed to carry birds through the air; and birds so use them. Legs and feet are constructed to carry animals across land, and animals do move about. Within these most broad divisions, however, are numerous smaller and more specialized adaptations. There are animals adapted to run swiftly, and animals adapted to protect themselves while moving more slowly—each according to its special way of life. The beaver specialized in water travel rather than on land, though it can also travel on land. Its feet, legs and many other organs are adapted to an amphibious (both land and water) existence, though its most special equipment is for an aquatic (water) way of life. Most interestingly, its hind feet are specifically adapted to work in water while its front feet are adapted for contact with solid objects.

Still more exciting, this vast array of specialization among living things functions together in a somewhat organized manner, resulting in mutual benefit to all. That is what makes possible the many forms we see in nature. For a very simple example: The willows, which serve the beaver as both food and building material, are adapted to grow in small stalks, in a wet habitat and with bark which is palatable and nutritious to beavers and a few other browsers. They provide nesting sites for some birds and cover for many small birds and animals. Beavers in turn benefit the willows by providing increased moisture in the soil around their ponds, and the beaver ponds conserve floating solids which build soil and thus still more willow habitat.

These many differing creatures—plant and animal—which live together in a locality, form an ecological community. Each kind fits into community life in the manner to which it is suited—biologists call it "niche." The beaver's adaptations qualify him well for his niche or role in his community. The system may be somewhat likened to an organized human society, where people with occupations perform their labors for the mutual benefit of all.

# Chapter Four

# PHYSICAL CHARACTERISTICS

Anything but regal, the beaver is about as shapely as a bag of blubber. This is partly due to his disproportionately large internal organs and partly to the layer of fat beneath his skin, which serves as insulation from the cold water. When standing upon all four feet, he appears like a giant brown mouse or rat. When he assumes other postures, however, his pauchiness prevails as it responds to the forces of gravity, thus belieing the animal's muscular, powerful and dexterous features. His wide, flat, and hairless tail immediately sets him apart from other members of his family.

## External Characteristics

**Size.** The largest of the rodent family, the beaver is one of very few animals capable of controlling its environment to some extent. The use of woody plants, including large trees, for both food and construction material, requires more size and strength than if the animal were only using herbaceous plants. To cut, drag, and place dam and lodge materials, to transport and cache a winter food supply, to cut ice and frozen dams in case of a winter freeze-in demands power. While a smaller beaver (or a similar animal) could become adapted to the use of small shrubs and build dams across very small streams, the ability to utilize both small and large plants and streams enlarges the environment suitable for beaver habitat. We might assume, then, that the beaver's present size is optimum for the conditions in which it lives.

But some beavers are much larger than others. This variation exists primarily because of the comparatively long life span—about 15 years—for an animal of this type. A good share of this life span is spent in the actual process of growing, though, of course the growth rate slows markedly with age, as in all mammals. In a study of beaver size relative to age, Grass and Putnam, working for the Wyoming Game and Fish Department, recorded the data shown on page 107. These data yield information regarding the wide variation in size among beavers. The size spread is actually greater than the table indicates, however, for there exist many extremes, both large and small. Vernon Bailey, working for the United States Biological Survey in 1921, captured a 110 pound beaver! On the small side, it is not uncommon to find eight-month-old cubs, usually the late-born of young pairs and perhaps the runts from extra large litters, weighing only 10 to 12 pounds after overwintering. External factors, such as climate, weather, food supply, litter size, and age or maturity of parents, governs beaver size, and this influence extends into maturity.

**Body Conformation.** Built like a blimp, the beaver's body (trunk) is short and broad; its legs stubby, powerful and widely spaced, the neck, very short and muscular; the chest and abdomen broad and deep. This structure, in addition to the large size, results in a large mass-to-surface-area ratio—an adaptation which conserves heat energy. The round to slightly oval shape of a beaver's skin prepared for the raw fur market also reflects the beaver's physique.

As a general rule, animal species inhabiting colder climates have shorter appendages (legs, feet, tails, noses) and bodies relative to size, as well as increased blood circulation to these organs. But the beaver's conformation is about the same in all climates of his extensive range, possibly because he lives in closer proximity to cold water than to any other factor in his external environment. However, some discernible *individual* differences occur among beavers. The males, for example tend to be more rangy than the females. The shape of the tail, which is to some degree genetically acquired, also varies from long and slender to short and broad.

**Incissor Teeth.** The adaptation and extensive development of incissor teeth, used for gnawing, are distinguishing characteristics of Order *Rodentia* (all rodents), with the beaver having developed these prominent "buck" teeth to their fullest. The beaver's lower incissors root far back in the mandible (jaw bone) and follow its curvature. The upper incissors have a much shorter root curvature, remaining anterior (in front) to the eye socket. (Since the beaver has no canine teeth, there is a gap—greatly enlarged by adaptation—between the incissors and the molars). These huge orange chisels are self-sharpening with use, and with them the beaver can cut off a willow the size of a man's finger in a single bite. They grow continually throughout the animal's life, which means that a beaver's teeth never wear out. This is not so in most

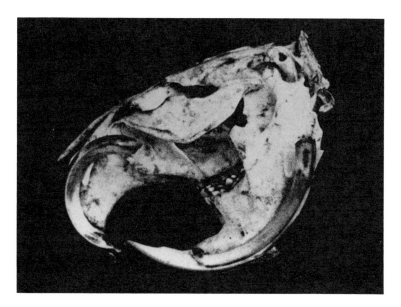

**The incissor teeth.**

This unskinned specimen shows lips close behind teeth, which permits underwater gnawing.

of the animal world. For example, grazing mammals live quite well until their teeth wear out, whereupon they soon die of malnutrition or starvation. The beaver, however, must maintain his incisors by wearing them down as fast as they grow or they will become too long, preventing the mouth from closing sufficiently for the molars to meet. The beaver would then die of starvation.

While trapping beavers in a small Wyoming stream, a drowning device failed and a large male beaver twisted out of the trap and escaped. Upon recapturing him about 18 months later, I noted he suffered from starvation. Examination revealed that one upper incisor had been broken off near the root (probably while fighting the trap), and because it fractured behind the growth area, it had failed to regenerate. The opposing lower tooth had continued to grow with nothing for it to wear away against, and upon growing more than an inch, the jaw was unable to close sufficiently to permit the molar to function. Fortunately, most escapes are preventable by proper placement of the trap, and the condition cited, is rare indeed.

The beaver's teeth are sharpened to the anterior or outside. This most important adaptation, permits an expansive penetration of the material being gnawed. As seen in the above photo, the upper and lower incissors do not meet directly, but the uppers overbite the lower teeth, which is characterisitc of not only rodents but man as well. In the gnawing process, the upper teeth hold still, while the lower teeth function as a pair of chisels, thus providing stability to the object being gnawed. (Eating an apple effectively demonstrates this method.)

**The Lips.** One who has only a casual acquaintance with the beaver may wonder why he keeps on "smiling" all the time. Not necessarily exemplifying happiness, the smile is produced because the lips do not close over the incissor teeth, but tightly behind them. This important adaptation to an aquatic-gnawing way of life permits the beaver to work under water without getting his mouth full of water.

**The Nose.** The extreme front (anterior) of the beaver—the nose, and its organs, nostrils, nose pad and whiskers—perform several important functions. The nostrils channel respiratory air to and from the lungs. The passageways are lined with membranes containing the olfactory nerves (sense of smell) which are capable of detecting certain air-borne chemical compounds and transmitting the information to the brain. With his olfactory apparatus, the beaver locates and sorts his food and discerns between friend and foe. Since open nostrils aggravate divers, humans have invented nose plugs to prevent water from entering the air passages. The beaver, however, is self-equipped; his nostrils are equipped with a pair of flap valves which close when he dives, swims or works beneath the water surface.

The bare nasal extremity around and between the nostrils is smooth, black, and a bit moist. This bare spot enhances the beaver's tactile sense, as more information can be gathered from bare skin than from skin covered by fur. A furry nose might also interfere with breathing. Except for these factors, adaptation might favor a furry nose for warmth.

The so-called whiskers, an arrangement of very coarse, stiff hairs, protrude from behind, below, and laterally from the nostrils for about three inches (about 3.5 cm). Their roots are connected to nerves and a very versatile set of muscles which can direct the whiskers at a number of angles, enabling the whiskers to detect objects near the sides of the face or head, e.g., a narrow passageway or some obstruction in the dark. They assist animals frequenting or living in burrows, but are also found on mammals who seldom, if ever, reside in dens.

**The Eyes.** The beaver's eyes are small, black and beadlike. Perceptually, the eye functions well for only small distances. Sight, however, is quite keen at close range, for it is most difficult to conceal an underwater trap from the trap-shy beaver. Also equipped for underwater work, the beaver can pull a thin transparent membrane over his eyeball like the goggles of a deep sea diver.

**The Ears.** Despite a small, rounded, external ear, the auditory sense of the beaver appears to be well developed. Since the beaver has but a rudimentary voice box, he communicates danger to fellow family members by slapping his tail upon the water. The signal is then received by audition. The ear, always alert to strange sounds, perceives all other danger signals.

**The Feet.** The front and hind feet of the beaver so vastly differ that one would scarcely believe they belong to the same species. The front feet are small, digitigrade (he walks upon the five digits), and dexterous with well developed digging claws. They grasp sticks and manipulate them to eat "corn-on-the-cob" style. The very large plantigrade (the animal walks with the heel flat to the ground) hind feet extend to the hock joint and are webbed for swimming. Completely exempt of fur, except for the dorsal surface which shows fine, very short (2 to 3 mm) fuzz, the skin of the hind feet is dark grey to black.

The preening toe—second from the inside—also exists on the hind foot and is unique for its double toe nail. This is the beaver's comb, which he uses to prevent his fur from matting and losing its waterproofing and insulating properties. By its aid, the

Close-up of the preening toe on the hind feet.

The legs are short, powerful and spaced widely apart.

beaver also remove's burrs and ectoparasites, such as fleas and lice, from his fur.

Because his hind feet adapt well to swimming, the beaver, like the duck, is awkward on land, making him vulnerable to attack by such predators as bears, wolves and lynx, when he ventures any distance from the safety of his moat of water.

**The Tail.** The beaver's tail consists of two quite different parts: the large, muscular and furry portion which joins the trunk and controls all the movements of the tail; and the flat, scaly distal part, generally thought of as the beaver's tail.

Beaver's tails vary greatly in shape from short and broad to long and narrow. Tail shape appears to be an individual or family trait like the nose of man. The dimensions given on page 106 are about average. The tail of the mature animal is about two inches (5 cm) thick at the edge of the fur, tapering to a quarter inch (about 6 mm) at the tip. Like the hind feet, this portion of the

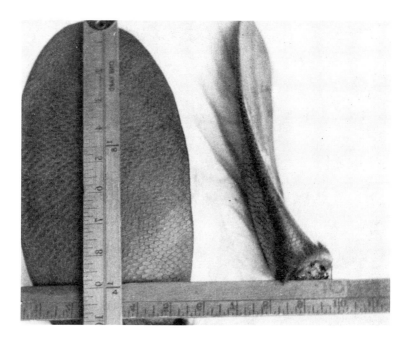

**The rough scaled beaver tail.**

beaver's tail is practically hairless. Here, the similarity ends, for black scales, similar to fish scales, heavily cover the thick skin of the tail, and a very sharp demarcation exists between the fur and scale. The fur of the muscular tail remains at full length and density right to this line, but on the hind leg it gradually becomes shorter until it finally just "peters" out on the foot.

Although somewhat trowel-shaped, the tail, contrary to popular belief, is not used as a trowel. Instead the tail is well adapted to perform three functions; it is used as a swim rudder, as a prop to balance the beaver while he works in an upright position, and as a paddle to signalize danger when slapped upon the surface of the pond.

**The Genital Organs.** Another unusual structure of the beaver is the external genitalia (sex organ), which features no visible difference between the sexes. Functions of elimination and reproduction are shared by a single opening. Being one who believes that each characteristic of all mammals either is or has been an adaptation pertinent to the species' survival, I think there must be a good reason for it. But what is it? The muskrat, which lives in quite similar environment, has quite typical rodent fixtures. And so do the mink and otter, of the *Mustela* group of carnivorous mammals. We might speculate, then, that it may have something to do with breeding behavior and thus facilitate the beaver's method of face-to-face copulation which will be described later.

Some of the internal differences between the sex organs, however are discernible through the external opening. The male's penis contains a bone (*os penis* or *baculum*) about one and a half inches long and about three eighths inch in diameter in the adult. Sexing the live animal can be accomplished by inserting a finger into the urogenital passage. In most cases the penis can also be felt by external palpation between the vent and the pelvis.

The oil from the oil glands, often observable by external examination, differs between the sexes. In the female it is light in viscosity and pale yellow in color, but in the male it is very viscous and copper brown. The ducts of these glands are located just within and at either side of the urogenital opening. Finger pressure on the gland will often cause it to exude a droplet of oil.

**Male genitals, oil glands and castors. Left, oil gland; left center, testicle; right center, os penis (with sheath cut away); right, castor.**

**Beaver Castors.** The castors and the oil glands are beneath the skin, on the exterior of the body cavity. These paired glandular structures lie parallel to each other in a thin muscle layer on each side of the vent. Their ducts open into the urogenital tract at the vent. By applying pressure at the sides, one can observe the ducts, which distend as small cones.

Encased in a translucent, convoluted heavy membrane, the pear-shaped castor lies just anterior to the torpedo-shaped oil gland. The dull orange to yellow castorium gives the external gland a pale yellow color. The consistency of the castorium might be said to resemble semi-dehydrated egg yolk. Its odor suggests that it contains terpenes and sulfur-bearing compounds. The gland is more active in the male, and becomes fuller and harder with age and maturity.

The castor's very pungent and long-lasting odor, when sufficiently diluted, transforms into a pleasant-smelling musklike aroma. Beaver trappers use it in conjunction with oil from the beaver's oil gland and such additives as oil of anise, turpentine, cloves, and whisky for luring beavers into their traps. Such scent formulas are held by many successful trappers in closest secrecy, but it is considered highly probable that "secret" formulas involve the use of beaver castor.

**The Oil Glands.** As previously indicated, the torpedo-shaped oil glands lie just posterior to the castor. They are encased in a pale pink convoluted membrane, and perhaps perform a more vital function to the survival of the species than the castors. They are the source of waterproofing for the beaver's fur. Though the animal is hydrophylic (water-loving), its fur must remain dry. A beaver with wet fur would be like a human with wet clothing. When insulating properties are lost, body heat (energy) drains rapidly away. So, like the duck and the wise virgins, the beaver must keep oil in his oiler—and keep oiling. This layer of oil also helps to keep the air trapped in the underfur while the beaver is under water—perhaps of importance equal to keeping the water away from the skin. The oil has a distinctive, pungent odor, slightly different between the sexes, and functions in sex communication as well as a waterproofing agent.

**The Mammary System.** The four mammae on the breast are distinguishing features of the beaver's mammary system. Development commences at about midpregnancy, and not long thereafter the teats become prominent through the fur. They recede again following the lactating period, which lasts about one month.

We can only speculate on the adaptive reasons for why they have only four mammae. Some biologists believe this limited number of teats (compared with other rodents and small mammals in general) effects the survivability of some of the members of large litters. However, I have seen litters of five in good condition and with no apparent difference in size among them, indicating a sharing of nipples during the nursing period. It would appear reasonable, however, that the number of teats do affect the survivability of young that reach weaning age.* We

---

* In swine, each piglet stakes a claim to a certain teat which it retains throughout the early nursing period, or until the family rejoins the communal swine herd. Then it is "first-come-first-served" at any teat on any sow as the lactating sows lie down in unison. In the mink, there appears to be a sharing system. I have seen female mink nursing litters of 6 to 7 young with only two lactating teats, but in some cases all eight teats are utilized by a litter of only two or three.

might also consider this: The population of various animal species remain about the same in the long run and more young are produced than can survive. The mortality of the excess young may be greater during the lactating period, or during over-wintering, or at some other critical period. Population restriction appears to be advantageous to the long-term survival of the species. Thus, it may be that the limited number of teats on the beaver controls the number of young beavers which survive the nursing period. Those which do survive are larger, with greater viability for the coming critical overwintering period.

**Females have no more than four teats though their litters may be larger.**

**The Fur.** The two kinds of fur that coat the beaver are the longer, coarser guard hair and the shorter, very fine underfur. The brown guard hair is from one and three-quarters to two inches long and varies in color from near beige to near black depending upon the individual beaver and geographic region. The darker types are to be found in the damp, cold, and shady regions, whereas the paler shades are favored in temperate and arid regions. Seldom, if ever, are the extremes in color shade found simultaneously in the same

**The length of the guard hairs is about two inches; the very fine underfur is about one inch deep in its natural slightly curly state.**

locality. The precise color shade we must attribute to individual color variation.

Though lighter, the underfur color blends with and compliments guard hair color. In its natural wavy condition, it is about half the length of the guard hair. Part of the beaver's fame is due to his underfur; because of its very fine texture and microscopic barbs, which cause a slight bonding together of the individual fibers, felt of the highest quality is produced from it.

The shedding and regrowth of fur splendidly exemplifies seasonal adaptation among mammals. It is well known that northern subspecies of beavers grow a heavier winter coat than their southern brothers. The adaptation is so well established genetically that an individual animal has little or no control over his coat change. For example an animal from a cold climate that is sent to a warm region will continue to grow heavy winter coats, and likewise an animal from a warm climate cannot readily adapt itself to the need for a heavy coat if sent to a cold territory.

Studies on the animal's change of pelage disclose interesting results. Experiments with the beaver and also different mammal species have indicated that the timing device for coat change is governed not by seasonal temperature changes, as was previously thought, but by the visual perception of the changing length of daylight hours.*

## Adaptations of the Internal Organs

A look inside this creature of wonders unfolds additional adaptations to its peculiar way of life. The Squire Beaver's paunchiness is not caused by overindulgence in riotous living, but by useful modification of some vital organs.

**The Digestive System.** The beaver's digestive system is designed to accommodate large quantities of indigestibles. Because the beaver will feast on a large amount of wood along with bark, herbs and grasses, the body must be able to handle and dispose of the junk in order to assimilate sufficient nutrients. The digestion problem is partially solved by an oversized stomach with a special gland near its top which contains an enzyme capable of reducing some of the cellulose to starch, which in turn, is subject to reduction to digestible sugar by other agents. The digestive system also sports a large convoluted "great colon" as well as a very large caecum (the large pouch forming the beginning of the large intestine) though this organ is not noticeably out of proportion to the caeca of other rodents or of lagomorphs (hares and rabbits).

The beaver is also known to eat some of its own fecal pellets, which are but partially digested, thus exposing the nutrients to a second bout with its digestive enzymes.

**Lungs and Liver.** The enlarged lungs and liver provide for extra functional capacity. The lungs store oxygen for use in underwater work (oxygen tank) and are capable of a very efficient oxygen exchange—75% compared to 15% to 20% for man's lung efficiency. (If man's oxygen-to-carbon dioxide exchange rate

---

* When pen-raising foxes, I once had a pup born without eyes. The lids and lashes were present, but there were no eyeballs. The fox was in otherwise excellent health. It grew to an abnormally large size, but failed to make the winter coat change. It just retained its fuzzy puppy fur without guard hair because its system could not recieve the signal to shed and regrow its coat.

**Part of the over-sized digestive system. 1. stomach; 2. liver; 3. great colon; 4. caecum.**

were as high as the beaver's, he would need lungs of only one fifth the size he now has, or would need to breathe only one fifth as often. He could also use his breath as a portable fire extinguisher, but it would be less than useless in coaxing a camp fire.) The enlarged liver serves as still another reserve oxygen tank, as well as a blood filter.

Because these internal organ adaptations increase oxygen supply and slow down the blood circulation and the metabolic rate while he is submerged, the beaver is capable of remaining and working under water for as long as 15 minutes.

**The Male Gonad.** Located near and parallel to the oil glands, the testicles lie beneath a layer of muscle. This is most unusual in mammals. All others with whom I am familiar, have an external pouch or scrotum which carry the testicles, because the spermatozoa are unable to withstand the higher temperature of the internal body. Why, then, does the beaver not require this protection? I speculate that perhaps a cooling device exists similar to the heat exchange mechanism described for the feet and tail, or that the beaver's body temperature is lower than in other mammals.

## Adaptations of Thermoregulation

**Conservation of Heat.** While the beaver has plenty of insulation to keep him warm, even during the winter months, it is often not realized that great amounts of body heat energy are required to keep his bare hind feet and tail warm. On the other hand, during the hot summer months the beaver often becomes the envy of all, as his natural inclination for swimming appears to be an easy and wonderful way to cool off. Few realize, however, that if he swam all day, his fur would become wet and matted and he would more than likely die of exposure. Since fur and fat insulate most of the beaver's body, heat has few avenues of escape.

The solution to these problems lies in a countercurrent blood vessel arrangement which aids the beaver to conserve heat or lose it as the external temperature demands. Adaptations whereby veins lie either close to or completely surround arteries conserve heat. Much of the heat from these arteries is diffused while passing by the cooled blood of the adjacent veins. In the hind leg, just above the foot where the leg is insulated by fur, the veins carrying the cooled blood from the foot separate into several small veins to completely and closely surround the leg artery, which has also separated into four smaller arteries. The venous (vein) blood is thus warmed and the arterial blood is precooled before entering the feet, thus preventing much body heat from escaping into the cold water. In the tail there are two such mechanisms—one on each side of the caudal vertebrae in the muscular portion, just forward from the bare tail, where it is insulated by both fur and fat.

**Release of Heat.** In each lower hind leg, there occurs one bypass vein located in the dorsal (top) side of the foot and continuing on up past the heat exchange area into the greater venous system without coming in contact or even close proximity with any arteries. Two bypass veins in the tail regulate blood flow to or around a heat exchange unit which runs laterally in each hemisphere of the muscular tail. The bypass veins carry the water-cooled blood back into the body systems rather than having it warmed by the arteries.

**Temperature Control Mechanism.** The venous blood returning to the interior of the body is shunted either to the heat exchange system or through the bypass veins by sphincter muscles associated with the walls of the veins. They either contract and constrict or relax and open the veins according to the needs of the animal, in response to signals initiated in the animal's brain.

Swimming all day during July or August is not required to keep the beaver reasonably cool. Merely submerging his tail and hind feet in cool water allows the beaver's thermoregulatory processes to work. We might liken this system to the cooling-heating system in an automobile with its combined radiator and thermostat, which keep the temperatures at a tolerable range, preventing extremes of either heat or cold.

## Chapter Five

# LIFE HISTORY

The beaver cub is born with a full coat of fur, teeth, and open eyes. About twelve inches (30 cm) long and weighing about 500 grams, or a little more than a pound, the beaver is capable of swimming soon after birth. The tunnels leading from the beavers' lodge to the pond are full of water, which reaches up close to the animal's living quarters. Water is therefore very close to the young beaver at all times, and young beavers are naturally attracted to it. They go down into it readily and often, but for the first few days of life are not strong enough to climb back out and up to the nest. Therefore, mother beaver is kept very busy rescuing her cubs from the tunnels. The same sharp teeth which cut down large trees are used in the tender rescue operation without harm to the cubs, as mother beaver opens her mouth very widely and encircles the abdomen of the cub behind those big incissors.

The young beaver begins to nibble leaves and twigs within a week or so following birth, while continuing to nurse its mother for about five weeks. During this time it will gradually develop the ability to subsist on a full vegetable diet.

Growth is rapid; the young cub increases in size about fifteenfold by fall—weighing about fifteen to seventeen pounds (about 7 to 8 kg)—and will be capable, should emergency demand it, of overwintering without the aid of his parents. At this age, however, he does not help with the heavy work of dam building or food storing. He remains at home, or within the family territorial boundaries, assisting with the work according to his capability, until just before his second birthday.

## The Reproductive Period

Just before its second birthday, the beaver leaves its home and family. A bit more than half grown, it spends the next year seeking a lifelong mate, locating and claiming a home site, building a home and protective pond, and preparing to produce its first offspring. One litter per year is produced throughout the reproductive period, estimated to be eight to ten years, though this may vary among beavers and localities.

## The Reproductive Season

The time in which breeding occurs, during midwinter, varies with geographic latitude and altitude, and often with the ages of the parent beavers. The young, first-time producers might engage in sexual activities as much as a month later than the mature pairs. From pen-raising of beavers, it has been determined that the gestation period averages about 110 days.

In its under-ice/snow winter quarters, the beaver is probably in total darkness. Another of nature's well guarded secrets is how it can time its breeding activities so precisely while being so isolated from daylight and weather conditions.

In a given locality and even a given region, beavers bear their young during the same time period. But surveying the continent, the time frame in which beavers give birth varies significantly and often coincides with the advance of springtime weather in a particular thermal line. In the Rocky Mountain region, for example, mature beavers have their young at about the time the buds break on the willows and the aspens. This creates a differential of five or six days per each altitude change of 1,000 feet (about 307 meters). Even this slight variation in time makes a noticeable difference in the sizes of the young when fall arrives. Those born earlier are significantly larger, and they remain larger throughout life. Thus, it appears that more favorable habitat produces larger beavers. Recent studies in the far north, however, indicate that some beavers wait an extra year before reproducing. These animals, by growing an extra year before the strain of reproduction, overcome the small-size handicap, but in doing so perhaps forfeit a year of reproductive life.

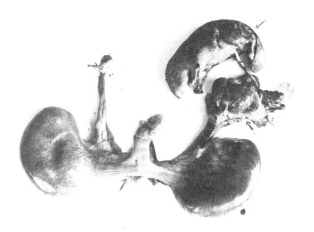

Female organs carrying three unborn young with one removed from uterus. Bottom arrow, duplex uterus; upper left, ovary; upper right, fetus removed from placenta; lower right, placenta.

## Productivity

The three-year-old sow (female) beaver produces but one or two young. She increases in productivity gradually with age, maturity, and perhaps environmental factors* until near the end of her reproductive age. While she has been known to produce as many as eight per litter (I have personally observed seven, but only once), and on occasion six, most mature sows produce three to five. Grasse and Putnam, in a study for the Wyoming Game and Fish Department, found the litter average to be 3.8. In more recent studies, however, the average is considerably lower, 2.9. The difference could be due to the younger ages of the sows sampled in the later studies.

---

* The physical factors of environment, as well as the food supply, could influence productivity. In population studies among beavers, it has also been observed that productivity tapers off as population pressures increase.

I have found no evidence of reduction of litter size as the sow passes the prime of life. Instead of a decrease in litter size, it seems that she stops producing quite suddenly. But for those who conceive in their later years, it has been asserted that they kill their young. I have seen no evidence of this myself.

## Life Expectancy

The longevity of a few beavers, held in captivity, has been observed. They have been known to live 17 years—rather long for a rodent. A more average life span is about fifteen years. The beaver may spend about ten of those years growing, although the rate of growth dramatically decreases in the latter period.

## Chapter Six

# BEHAVIOR

### Gnawing

Gnawing, one of the beaver's most elementary and compulsive acts, is perhaps the most distinguishing behavioral charactristic of *Order Rodentia,* but developed to its utmost by the beaver. Gnawing makes possible the beaver's way of life, for the habit not only processes the animal's food and building material, but also keeps his tools sharp and worn to proper length.

Anyone who examines the works of the beaver will be convinced that it makes a fetish of gnawing upon almost everything gnawable. Its choice of wood upon which to gnaw is governed by availability and palatability, not upon the beaver's ability to gnaw it. He'll tackle a poplar tree—one of his favorite dishes—of almost any size and will generally work at it alone, though pair work has been observed upon occasion. Biologist, Vernon Bailey, of the former United States Biological Survey, found a beaver-gnawed cottonwood stump in Montana measuring 46 inches in diameter.

When felling trees or willows, the beaver sits upright on his hind legs and uses his tail for a balancing prop. If the tree is large, he will gnaw all the way around it unless it is on a steep hillside, in which case he'll confine his work to the upper side of the tree. In

While gnawing off a tree, the beaver stands upon its hind feet, braces or balances with its tail and uses the front feet to stabilize the work. Photo by Bailey.

the felling process, he will turn his head to one side and make cross-grain cuts three to four inches apart then split out the chip before repeating the process. A beaver might spend several nights falling a tree, even as small as eight to ten inches in diameter, though it could be accomplished easily in a few hours. Sometimes the project is abandoned without apparent reason. When cutting willows, the beaver grasps them with his front paws and manipulates them as he desires. Willows are felled in any desired direction, but trees must be left to wind and chance, resulting in some crisscrossing and lodging among standing trees.

## Oiling the Fur

All four feet share the habitual and vital chore of oiling the fur—each foot servicing an area of the body not accessible to the others. The beaver simply applies a paw to his vent, exudes a drop of oil into it and brushes lightly—with the flow of the fur. In the process the beaver's roly-poly physique assumes all sorts of unusual—even comical—postures and appears to suffer no discomfort. Whether the beaver actually senses a need for waterproofing, or whether he merely enjoys such grooming, the behavior is as necessary to his survival in his aquatic habitat as eating.

## Building

The beaver has earned considerable fame in man's world as a construction expert. It is a compulsive builder of dams and lodges in the portions of its range where building is feasible. The purpose of any construction by animals is for a measure of control of their environment. The bird's nest is a shelter, as is the burrower's den. The beaver has advanced still farther in environmental control systems.

**Dam Construction.** In their studies for the Wyoming Game and Fish Commission, Grasse & Putnam (1955) observed one small stream where there were no beavers and none had previously resided. There they planted five unmated beavers of each sex. The following year, all had chosen mates, established five distinguishable colonies, and had constructed fifty-five dams! One large dam per pair would have secured for them the necessary homesite and water depth. Why, then, should these pioneers build eleven dams (average) per pair the first season? One becomes tempted to speculate that the beaver possesses the humanlike characteristic of wanting to grab all the property he can. We shall soon see, however, that the enlarged territory serves a beneficial purpose to both beaver family and species.

The purpose of the dam is security, not only from predators, but from ice as well. The "home" dam must impound sufficient water depth to insure that the ice of winter does not threaten to isolate the food cache or seal off the tunnels between the lodge and the food behind the dam. The family assembles during the fall to build the food cache and to spend the winter. Any other dams built by the family supplement the home dam. Though not absolutely essential to the survival of the beaver, the additional dams serve the beaver in that an enlarged territory increases the food supply for that family, enhances safety, facilitates water

A very wide beaver dam (about 50 feet) on a river flooded by high water.

transportation of food and building materials, and probably inhibits the too-close settlement of competing neighbors. The supplementary dams, then, serve for convenience, territorial expansion, and safer dispersion of family activities as a result of additional moats. These auxiliary ponds become especially convenient during springtime when the sow expels all other family members from the lodge and its immediate surroundings, including the home pond.

Thus, we might conclude that the beaver exhibits an inherent compulsion to structure a protective home environment, and that this compulsion is met by the beaver's keen ability to execute such a structure—even with a minimal water supply.

How, then, does the beaver build his dam? He has left unconcealed a few dam building secrets, available to any careful observer. To start a new dam, he cuts a green willow, carries it with and between his teeth/mouth into the edge of the stream and lays a rock upon it to prevent its floating away. Usually, several willows are placed close together in the same manner—lengthwise with the stream current and the butt ends facing downstream. If the stream bottom has no rocks in it, the beaver uses mud to anchor the willows. It carries mud and rocks in its arms; willows/wood with its teeth.

Construction begins near the bank on the side of the stream where there is the least amount of water current. The beaver might build up one side of the dam to above water level, then the other side, before blocking the current in the middle of the channel, or he might build a foundation clear across the stream and evenly add willows to the top of that. The method depends upon the location in the channel and the nature of the stream's current, upon the size of the stream and perhaps also upon the whim of the builder.

After the first sticks are secure, the next ones are placed both crosswise and quartering against the upstream ends of the first layer of sticks, where they are anchored in place. There is usually a mixture of trimmed and untrimmed willows. From this point, no consistently perceivable placement pattern is maintained except in one location—a most important one—the lower side of the dam. There, the beaver places numerous sticks so that one end points downstream and subsequently becomes incorporated into the fabric of the dam. These sticks serve as braces, or props, which prevent the dam from being pushed downstream by the force of the impounded water. The structure upstream from the braces becomes a haphazard network of sticks, stones, mud, leaves—anything which might be available and movable to the site. The coarser material is placed first to serve as a framework and progressively smaller sticks and twigs mingled with rocks, mud and leaves are placed in front. The apparent logic of this method is that there is not as much water pressure against the dam while it is leaky and unsealed and its basic framework is being established. Finally, it is sealed with mud which is excavated from needed tunnels and burrows as well as dredged from the bottom of the impoundment. The mud is often several feet thick at the base of the dam, but just barely sealed at the top of the dam. The sealing often varies in degree to regulate the rate of the stream's flow through the impoundment, i.e., a very small stream inflow requires a tight seal all of the way to the top of the dam, but a large stream inflow requires that a large amount of water be let through the top of the dam, so the seal isn't made too tight. If it were, there would be danger of earth erosion around

A very high beaver dam. From Wyoming Game & Fish Commission Bull. No. 6.
Grasse & Putnam, authors.

the end of the dam or through a bend in the stream, or the dam
itself may be washed out.

There are limits to beavers' dam building capabilities, i.e.,
they cannot successfully dam streams which are too large or too
swift. Most streams thirty to fifty feet (10 to 17 meters) across can

A beaver dam located to provide maximum water impoundment with minimum construction. Note the vertical placement of sticks and poles behind the dam for bracing against the water pressure. From Wyo. Game & Fish Commission Bull. No. 6.

A very strong beaver dam. It is unusual that a dam can withstand the high waters of spring runoff on such a large stream.

be dammed in the fall, when the water flow is at its lowest. If the dam is built tightly, and higher than the stream banks, flooding occurs, and stream bottomlands are placed under water. If these flooded stream bottomlands are covered with willows, it is not unusual for the beavers to extend the dam out among the willows, raising the water level still higher, eventually resulting in a dam across the entire bottomland and up to a quarter mile (almost ½ km) in length. This creates a series of small, shallow waterways among the willow bushes (which are often a feature of streambottom lowlands), affording greater waterway access to food, as well as an extended barrier to predators.

Long, high dams often arch or curve upstream, adding strength to the structure to resist the water pressure of the impoundment. I have yet to see one curving downstream, which would have a decided structural weakness.

A beaver dam appearing to be made of rocks. It may be that a dam of willows and rocks was constructed at this site a number of times and that the willow sticks have rotted away, leaving the accumulated stones.

Beavers can seldom dam extremely swift streams unless they are very small. Also steep grades may prevent the construction of a sufficiently large pond area. If a large stream moves rather slowly during low runoff, but swiftly when high, the dam built during the fall will usually wash out the following spring. This is not a serious problem for the beaver, however. The dam has already served its important function of protecting the food cache and will merely be replaced again before the next caching time. On streams like these, beavers seldom bother building auxilliary dams. Rapidly flowing mountain streams would thus appear to be poor beaver habitat, except if there is a good food supply a large beaver population is often attracted.

Beavers sometimes subject small and swift streams to permanent damming. They build during low water flow. In some small, steep canyons of the Rocky Mountain region, dams are sometimes constructed up to ten feet high—the beaver's answer to the steep-grade problem.

While beavers prefer to work with willows—probably because they are the most abundant woody shrubs—almost anything can be used as dam building material. Many dams are constructed entirely of aspen. I have even seen a few made of sagebrush and a few rocks, and two partial dams composed entirely of rocks. On streams which flow near cornfields, dams are sometimes built of cornstalks when willows are scarce.

**Lodge Construction.** For the growing beaver family, building a house, or lodge—both words are used to describe the beaver's abode—takes precedence over other activities. This is especially true for beavers residing in low swampy areas if they are to maintain dry living quarters. However, some terrain—such as streams with high, steep banks—are not conducive to house-building. In such places, the beavers will rely upon a few bank dens, one of which is large enough to accommodate the entire family. Where feasible though, pairs will construct a house—be it ever so humble that it is scarcely noticeable—as soon they have a suitable pond. Like the feudal lords of old, building a castle with a moat around it, the beavers do likewise, except that they construct the moat first.

The construction of the dome-shaped lodge is not as

A very large beaver lodge. Photo by Vernon Bailey.

complicated as we might suspect, but its very simplicity illustrates the animal's ingenuity. The beavers pile up a mound of sticks, mud, and other materials over the air vent of a bank den with an underwater opening, then dig, gnaw, and chew, their way up through the middle of the mound. Employing the same technique and reaching a sufficient altitude above water to ensure a dry nest, they excavate a room large enough to be used by the entire family for all indoor living needs. In the area chosen for sleeping quarters, they build a soft nest of finely shredded dry wood. The other part of the room functions as a combined living and dining area; in the summertime, a feeding area for the young; in the winter, for the entire colony.

The beaver shingles the exterior of the lodge with mud, except for a very small area at the top of the structure which is left for ventilation. When cold weather freezes the structure solidly, this further shields the beaver from hungry predators; the only access to the living quarters occurs through the underwater tunnels leading to the pond and the food cache.

The lodge, as first built by the young beaver pair, stands small—often no more than about two feet (.6m) high and some four feet (1.3m) in diameter. As the family grows, they enlarge the house by adding materials to the exterior and gnawing out a larger interior. They often make any additions quite evenly in all dimensions, but some beavers build their lodges higher and narrower than do others, which could perhaps be attributed to increased dam height with its consequent higher water level. Should the family reside at the same address for a number of years, the house might be built up to six feet (2 m) high and a dozen feet (approximately 4 m) in diameter. Most beaver lodges never attain such size, however. A five by ten foot (1.6 x 3.3 meter) house is a fairly large one.

The number of entrance tunnels the beaver constructs from pond to lodge—all under water—varies and depends upon the particular site, whether the lodge is partially or fully surrounded by water, and perhaps upon preference. The beaver has been known to build as many as five entrance tunnels but probably never less than two, as he is too wise to be caught without an escape route should an enemy appear in his doorway. Auxilliary tunnels also provide good insurance against freeze-in during cold weather.

**Cut-away drawing of a beaver lodge, with one of the tunnels shown.**

**Canal Systems.** The beaver lodge and winter food cache are located near each other at the main pond. This pond is often sufficiently impounded to raise the water level to approximate the stream-bank level. In such cases beavers sometimes construct canals lateral to the stream channel (or length of pond). The excavations may be from one to two feet wide and deep enough, in relation to the pond level, to hold from six inches to a foot of water. These structures are either newly constructed by the contemporary beaver family or remodeled canals of previous beaver colonies. The canals are usually situated between the beaver's home and a major food source located at such a distance from the main pond that the beaver would find it difficult if not impossible, to transport the food home without the aid of a canal system. Actually, bay would a more proper term for the system, as it has no outlet and usually no inflow.

A beaver canal constructed on grade to assist in water transportation of food and building materials.

## Construction Engineering

Even more remarkable than the beaver's ability to build structures which yield so much control over his environment, rests his ability to employ sound engineering principles in both construction and selection of construction sites. In choosing dam sites, outlets to already-existing ponds and lakes require insignificant thought, but meandering streams demand full consideration. Riffles, for example, must be contended with. Dams are built above the riffle, not below it, and where there exists a series of riffles, the dam is erected above the first one. This practice results in maximum water impoundment for a minimum expenditure of material and effort.

The selection of the lodge site also requires consideration. Ideally, a location at the tip of a narrow peninsula and adjacent to the deepest water in the impoundment provides maximum water protection around the lodge as well as sufficient water depth, which allows an ice-free food cache to remain close to the lodge. The beavers select a site as near this ideal as possible and then remodel its shortcomings as much as geography will permit. In some locations the project may require years of summertime labor.

As indicated previously, beavers construct canals in which to transport materials, especially heavy products growing some distance lateral to the main pond and lodge. Commenced at water edge and level, and constructed on a water grade the full length, the canals attain a surprising uniformity of water depth.

## Food and Feeding

The beaver selects food plants by choice and availability. Willows (Silax spp.) constitute the mainstay of his diet, but not by first choice. In other words, willows are the beaver's bread and potatoes, but not his cake. While there are many willow varieties, it does not appear that the beaver prefers one over another.

Poplars are the beaver's first choice of food, with aspen (Populus tremuloides) as the most favored poplar. These shimmery-leafed, smooth, pale-barked trees grow on hillsides where the soil is fairly rich and deep. One seldom finds them growing within a quarter mile of good beaver habitat, because the beavers keep them trimmed back.

The narrow-leafed cottonwood (*P. angustifolia*) predominates along swift-flowing western river valleys. Beavers feed upon them, though not as extensively as the aspen. This is partially due to the generally high and dry banks and swift gravel-ridden streams—the habitat in which cottonwoods thrive. However, such habitat proves less desirable to the beaver because of excavation problems in coarse gravel.

The plains, black and eastern cottonwoods, as well as the Lombardy poplar, are presumably palatable to the beaver. Beavers also cut mountain alder (*Alnus tenuifolia*) for food. Interestingly, they seem to shun both the black hawthorn (*Craetagus douglasii*) and the water birch (*Betula occidentalis*), large deciduous shrubs inhabiting some stream banks of the Rocky Mountains. Though many streams run near and even among conifers, the tree is seldom touched by the beaver. Pioneer beaver ponds (those being established for the first time in a locality) often submerge the roots and drown Colorado spruce (*Picea pungens*), a conifer very common along mountain stream bottoms, but the beaver does not eat any of the tree. Nor do they ever eat subalpine fir (*Abies lasiocarpa*), douglas fir (*Pseudotsuga* spp.), engleman spruce (*Picea englemanii*), or ponderosa pine (*Pinus ponderosa*). While lodgepole pine (*Pinus contorta*) are felled by beavers on rare occasions, they are used for neither food nor building material. The beaver will cut and use giant sagebrush for dam building material, but not for food.

Why does a beaver often travel hundreds of yards from home to select food—certain willow stalks, for example—when willows are growing all about the main pond? Does the beaver systematically examine and classify according to desirability every willow bush in its domain? These questions, among others, are difficult to answer. There is one question, however, which we can more profitably speculate upon: Why doesn't the beaver simply girdle* the bark from trees and other food plant stalks for as high as he can reach instead of felling and dragging them before eating the bark from them? An unwritten law seems to prohibit beavers from gnawing the bark from a standing stalk or tree trunk. Even lone beavers who winter without food cache (and this is not uncommon) and tunnel beneath deep snow to

---

* To remove a band of bark completely from the circumference of a tree.

willow bushes first cut the stalks, then cut off lengths as they pull the stalk down through the snow, and finally peel the lengths in the conventional horizontal position rather than girdling the upright stalk.

So, again, why does the beaver avoid girdling tree bark? Could it be that he understands girdling actuates the waste of most of the edible food material since the stalk would die and commence to wither in a few days, and that the long-term result would be less food and, consequently, less beavers? Futhermore, dead willow patches would characterize stream bottoms and the entire biotic community would be adversely affected. Obviously, then, it would be maladaptive for the beaver to girdle its food plants and leave them to waste. But does the beaver know this and behave accordingly? There is *no* evidence that he does. A better explanation suggests that he merely prefers the tender tops, twings and branches to the main stalks. By felling the stalk, the beaver gains access to what he wants. After consuming the preferred parts he may then eat some of the bark rather than looking for an entirely new stalk, a habit which is ecologically beneficial.

An interesting last observation of food plant selection by the beaver concerns the lone aspen growing in the midst of a willow thicket near a beaver establishment—not an uncommon sight in the mountains. As mentioned, the beaver favors the aspen over the willow. Surprisingly though, the beaver will not cut the willows for access to the aspen; they are incapable of making the calculations, as smart as they appear to be. If they don't want those particular willows surrounding the aspen, they apparently consider the tree inaccessible to them.

**Cutting and Transporting Food.** The felling or cutting for food correlates with the felling of woody plants for building, as previously described. In fact, beavers add food residue to both dam and house. While beavers graze and consume grass and clover where they find it, they transport woody plants by dragging or floating them to a preselected site—a place familiar, convenient and safe. The entire family may partake of the "imported" meal near the lodge, or the foodcutter may prefer to dine in solitude and choose a place accordingly. Any excess food remains at the feeding site to be consumed as a "leftover" the following day.

**Feeding sites.** While beavers usually dine in shallow water, on occasion they eat on land near water. Protected coves upwind from the large pond where the water is about six inches deep, are favorite feeding sites. On one side the cove water protects the beaver from approaching predators, and the wind alerts him to enemies from the other side. Favorite sites for solitary dining are at the lower end of an island. In these locations, feeding usually takes place above water level on the gravel bar. If amateur trappers disturb him, the beaver simply vanishes—leaving no sign of his whereabouts. He goes elsewhere, feeds in stream riffles, and the current carries the telltale residue away.

Feeding sites are subject to change with season. In early spring the adult male goes exploring for fresh food in lieu of cache food (see Food Storage). He travels beneath the ice of ponds and over the dams, which requires that he cut some ice to emerge below the dams and re-enter the water above them (or visa versa when traveling downstream)—unless the winter has been mild enough to permit a bit of thawing at dam's edge. A snow trail must also be broken over the dam. But this is the extent of his snow trail on the stream bottom; he never makes one across pond ice. The journey may take him as far as a half mile from home then up a hillside through deep snow for a hundred yards or more to an aspen grove. If there are no aspens to be had, the beaver may settle for a fresh willow bush. Then he finds a riffle, or other ice-free water, where he eats his fill before returning home. The other family members must find their own fresh sticks or eat stale cached food.

In many years of beaver trapping, I have never taken an adult or adolescent female far from home before the ice break-up. They remain at the lodge and dine in it and the entrance tunnels, utilizing the cache for food source. Soon after the ice breaks the near two-year-olds leave, the yearlings feed singly wherever they may, and the adult female remains at the lodge and feeds nearby while awaiting the arrival of her new litter of young. As soon as the new litter attains sufficient age, the parents carry fresh twigs to them each day while they remain inside the lodge. As they grow older, they feed in the shallows near the house. They may feed at a family feeding site further from the lodge by early fall. Periods of cold weather during spring or fall cause beavers to retract feeding activities to the vicinity of the lodge.

Unless beavers feed in concealment or on stream riffles, their feeding sites are easily recognized by the residue of peeled, near-white sticks. The numbers of these sticks may indicate the size of the beaver family.

**The Feeding Event.** Beavers are nocturnal, but may occasionally be seen at any time of day. The most usual time of first emergence for the evening meal follows shortly after sunset, though it may vary somewhat among families and whether they have been disturbed by men or predators. The adult male usually appears first, but sometimes a younger beaver precedes the adult. The adult male initially tests the air with both ears and nose and, if no unusual sounds or odors are detected, he proceeds to secure his evening meal and tend to other chores, such as dam inspection and a visit to the scent mound (see Communication). Other family members soon follow, though each may go his own separate way to obtain food or pursue other interests.

Should the emerging adult male discover an intruder or a suspicious sound or odor, he slips quietly beneath the water and returns to the lodge to "spread the word." He may then venture out and swim beneath the water to an overhanging willow bush, or some other object of concealment, and raise his head above water to test the air. Until the threat has passed, the beaver won't expose himself on the open pond. All other family members remain inside until it is safe to emerge. If the disturbance has been of a serious nature, they do not emerge until after dark.

Emerging beaver families exemplify a diversity of behaviors as they prepare for the feeding event. Some adults are naturally shy or may have experienced adversities at one time which now make them very cautious and easily disturbed, while other adults are quite fearless, of man, at least. The reactions of parents transfer to the young. Thus, the family behaves unitedly in response to disturbances.

Full feeding activities gain momentum after darkness settles. Then the entire family "bark" sticks simultaneously; the sound of teeth in bark may be heard for up to a hundred feet (30 m) or more. An observer must approach carefully from downwind and *never* snap a twig.

**Food Requirement.** Experiments have shown that a twenty-six pound (11.8 kg) beaver requires 850 kilocalories (kilo=1000) of energy per day to maintain its weight. This energy may be derived from 1.5 pounds of aspen food (about 567 kcal/lb.) or food plants which have similar energy values. To maintain a maximum growth rate this same animal will require 2040 kilocalories of energy per day, or about 3.6 lbs. (1.63 kg.) of aspen.

A man moderately exerting himself over an eight-hour period requires about 1900 kcal. to perform his work. He requires an additional 1400 kcal. for eight hours of non-work and 500 kcal. for eight hours of sleep, totaling 3800 kcal. per day. A hard-working man requires 6200 kcal. Now, if we assume the man weighs seven times as much as the beaver (7 x 26 = 182 lbs.), an energy per pound of body weight comparison can be made, as below.

## Comparison of Energy Requirements of Beaver and Man

|  | Body Wt. (lbs.) | Req./24 Hrs. | Kcal/lb. |
|---|---|---|---|
| Non-growing Beaver | 26 | 850 kcal | 32.7 |
| Growing Beaver | 26 | 2040 kcal | 78.5 |
| Moderately Working Man | 182 | 3800 kcal | 20.9 |
| Hard Working Man | 182 | 6200 kcal | 34.1 |

---

* An acre of aspen has been calculated to yield 5840 pounds of food for about 3.3 million kcal. of energy.

**Food Storage.** Providing food for winter is another well-known behavioral characteristic of the beaver. Other mammals, such as the tree squirrels and minks, share the urge to hoard food. Nevertheless, the beaver's remarkable method of storing food as a family project attests to its high level of intelligence and adaptation to a harsh winter environment.

To create a food store, the beaver finds or prepares a deep hole in the pond near the house where there is little or no current to wash the cache away. Beavers living in larger streams also make their caches though they have no dam. In these locations the cache might be held in place by a brush obstruction, such as a willow snag hanging into the stream, or by a large boulder, or it might be placed in the dead-water corner of an eddy.

When fall approaches the beaver begins to build his food cache by simply putting a pile of green willows or poplars on top of the water at a desired site. When he adds materials to the original pile the weight pushes the pile down. A food cache is not complete until it reaches the bottom of the pond.

Caches vary in size—in both depth and circumference—and occasionally, a family will make two caches close by each other. Unlike the material in the dams and the house, only select ingredients go into the food cache. Willows, being the most prevalent food plant, are the staff of life. But beavers dearly love poplars. If available, the beavers store aspen in the cache. They will go out of their way to gather it. They will transport it a quarter of a mile or more, even if this entails going upstream some distance, then up a steep hillside to reach the grove. They fell the trees and log them into transportable lengths, take a log with their teeth and drag it homeward. The workers use the same route each trip, so a well-defined trail soon results. The drag trail runs straight down the hill, not necessarily toward the cache, but toward water, for water is used as much as possible to transport logs and sticks. The beaver, upon reaching water, converts himself from drag-horse to tug. To prove that he deems water transportation safer and more economical than land transportation, he engineers the lateral canals as far in the direction of the food source as the water level will permit.

Beavers seldom drag food for the cache uphill because of the difficult work involved, but tend to accumulate food from levels higher than the lodge before exploring downstream for storage edibles. Rather than gather from below his house, the beaver will move and build a new lodge and pond just below a fresh food source. The distance of the move will depend upon the location of abundant food, the adaptability of the terrain to a homesite, and the availability of unclaimed territory (see Territorial Behavior).

Beavers evidence some division of labor at food storing time—not the result of a rigid social order, but rather the result of individual maturity and experience. For example, the parent beavers range farthest from home and fell the trees far up on the hillside, while yearlings work nearer the home pond. The cubs remain near the lodge and do little or no work contributing to the survival of the colony.

To some extent, the size of the food cache will reflect the number of beavers in the colony, but it cannot be relied upon as an accurate indicator. Nor can one foretell the severity of the coming winter from the size of the beaver's food cache. For example, if one adult beaver falls victim to predation or disease, very little caching might occur, which by no means depicts either the kind of winter ahead or the number of animals, but rather challenges the hardy and resourceful beaver to gather food throughout the winter. I have often wondered why they go to the trouble of storing food for winter when they can effectively tunnel beneath the snow to willow bushes, where they either feed or drag willows back to the pond or house. The answer is that caching provides security and saves heat energy, permitting the animals to winter in better physical condition.

Beavers who fail to provide an adequate winter food cache rarely feed above snow in wintertime because of the difficulty in moving about in loose snow, the cold temperatures, and their vulnerability to attack by predators. Occasionally, where beavers reside near an open spring (a spring, at its source, is much warmer than a stream in midwinter and does not freeze over for some distance depending on its volume), they will feed or cut from on top of the snow as soon as it becomes solid enough to support their weight. This practice discredits the intelligence of the usually cautious beaver, for winter is the time when predators are

A profusion of willows, the beavers' bread and butter, are growing at this advanced pioneer stage beaver pond.

exceptionally hungry, prey is scarce, and cover most sparse.

Under normal conditions, when the cache is complete and cold weather arrives, the beaver merely dives out to the cache, grasps a branch and returns with it to the dining room. The inedible portion he shoves out beneath the ice, and it eventually becomes a part of the dam. But a filled cache doesn't take all of the work out of winter. Beavers must continue gnawing on something, and the never-ending chore of oiling their fur demands attention as well. Their premises require regular inspection, for the thickness of the ice could threaten the cache and house tunnels leading to it, especially during winters when only light snowfall occurs and the pond is insufficiently insulated from the frigid air. When this happens, the beaver cuts the top of the dam just enough to permit the water level to drop a few inches, which creates a dead air space that serves as insulation. The ice which forms beneath the space will remain thin, thus preventing overicing and freezing off of the access tunnels.

## Communication

How does the beaver identify and communicate with other beavers? With its rudimentary vocal development, it no doubt makes some communicative sounds and, as previously indicated, it transmits a danger signal with a slap of its tail upon the pond surface. The sense of sight appears to play a minor role in beaver communication, while most communication seems to take place via the olfactory sense. With its nose the beaver receives the chemical messages sent by the castorium and oil glands of other beavers. This system, not as simple or primitive as it at first appears, serves the purposes of the beaver quite well.

The beaver castorium has long been recognized by fur trappers as a principle attractant to other beavers. Biologists also have concluded that castorium acts as a messenger of friendship to family members and a warning to strange beavers not to tresspass. Other observers claim that castorium contains an aromatic sex indicator. Some say that the chemical composition of the castorium of each individual beaver is sufficiently different to be recognized by the odor, and is thus the agent by which individual beavers are distinuished one from another. I personally view some of these conclusions skeptically, and I'll explain why below.

It has been observed that adult males pay most attention to the odor of the castorium of strange males, but only slightly less attention to that of strange females. The reactions vary from sniffing about, indicating perhaps mild interest, to hissing and tail slapping, which might be interpreted as expressions of anger. Adult females demonstrate some interest in strange castorium, but less than the males. Young beavers demonstrate little or no interest. Surprisingly, castorium appears to have little attraction to beavers except during the springtime, principally April and May.

From personal observations, I conclude that though the castorium could perhaps be used for individual recognition by other beavers, it is not the primary conveyor of individuality. Rather it is used to communicate messages left at selected sites (see The Scent Mound) for other beavers to "read." We must conclude, then, that though it does have its place, castorium could scarcely be considered to be the beaver's most important chemical messenger.

The chemical composition of castorium, includes terpenes and related compounds, ingredients of the essential oils of plants, the odors of which are believed to function as attractants to some forms of life and repellents to others. Other castor ingredients probably comprise some sulfur-containing compounds, perhaps some of the higher mercaptans (organic molecules in which the oxygen atoms are replaced by sulfur atoms). The lower mercaptans—those with small molecules—smell very foul, such as in skunk musk. Beaver castor attracts a number of species and probably repels none. There can be little doubt that its purpose is to influence behavior.

**The Oil.** In addition to waterproofing himself, the beaver utilizes the oil from his anal oil gland to communicate, which is evidenced by the differences between male and female anal oil and from observed beaver reactions to the differences. The male's oil is extremely viscous and of a dark copper brown color with a strong and distinctively "masculine" pungency, while the female's is less viscous, a pale yellow color, and somewhat sweeter and more "feminine" in odor. This is not to imply great differences between the sexes in the odor of the anal oil, because they are really quite similar—both related somewhat to the odor of the castorium.

My experience is that oil is perhaps of greater and more individualized importance than castorium because the oil is applied very frequently, often to the entire fur surface. Water resistant, it remains on the beaver during and after swimming. In other words, it is ever present with each individual—as permanent as the human countenance—and possibly may even be detected on top of the beaver's head while it is swimming. It might well be termed the individual beaver's social security number; with it he is accepted in the family, but without it, or if it is strange or unfamiliar to the adult residents, he will be driven from the colony.

Though there is no way to prove that the oil carries individualized odor, I have often used it exclusively to lure beavers on the trapline as a sexually dimorphic substance. When using male oil, I captured almost all male beavers; and when using female oil, a majority of the take were females, but also a considerable number of males. My explanation is that males tend to be more "snoopy" than females, but a better explanation might be that since males emerge from the dens or lodges earlier in the evening than the females, they reach the traps first. In capturing trap-shy beavers, I have used the oil of a mature animal liberally as a lure.

## Beaver Scent Mounds

Human awareness of the beaver scent mound may reach almost as far into antiquity as our awareness of the beaver. The mound was used as a trap site soon after the invention of the steel trap and was probably the basis for the subsequent concoction and use of scent lures.

To create the foundation of a scent mound, a beaver dredges and carries an armful of sediment—mud, sticks, leaves—from the bottom of the pond, deposits it upon the pond bank, and straddles atop it, where he leaves his "signature," a mixture of castorium, oil and urine. Other beavers of the same colony subsequently add to the scent mount in like manner. Mounds of up to two to three feet in diameter, and more than a foot high, are not uncommon in areas where the same family members have remained undisturbed and added to the original scent mounds for a number of seasons. However, no correlation exists between the number or location of mounds in a family area and the number of beavers in the colony. Nor do they appear to be placed according to any specific plan or preconceived design, though most are located at the edge of the main pond and near shallow water—perhaps for the sake of ease in dredging up the mound building material from the shallows. Unlike the wolf's scent posts, the beaver's scent mounds do not circumscribe the family's range.

The function of the scent mound is controversial. Heretofore believed a territorial boundary marker (see Territorial Behavior) to "shoo" transients and neighbors away, this assumption is now in question, partly due to the confusion of two terms—"territory" and "home range"—and partly from the observation that family members make a social event out of using them. Another problem to be reckoned with is whether urine has a communicative value. Some investigators who claim a social value—even individual identity—to castorium ignore the possible role of urine, which is mixed with castorium as it is placed on the scent mound. It has been determined that there is wintertime sexual dimorphism in fox urine. Why not beavers, as well? For all we now know, urine may carry some of the keys to individual identity and could be as laden with information as the castorium. We may be quite certain of one thing: The scent mound has a social function and the information is carried by castorium, oil, or urine or all three.

Another interesting aspect of the scent mound is that it is used primarily during springtime, mostly during April and May. This period coincides with the migration and mate-seeking activities of the two-year-olds, who at this time of year have left home. Thus, there are usually many transient beavers traveling along the waterways (see The Plight and Adventures of Two-Year-Olds). A right of way through claimed beaver family ponds is accorded to these travelers. They go upstream and down, apparently in in relative peace, but are not permitted to tarry. Perhaps the scent mound warns the transients that certain premises belong to someone else and they had best keep moving. This could be what provides for an orderly and relatively peaceful distribution of the beaver population while protecting established family units from the adverse effects of overcrowding.

## Exploitation of Beaver Behavior

Using castorium as a base, beaver trappers have developed an array of lures or scents in attempting to increase their catches and to out-trap competitors. Supposedly magic, but sacredly secret, scent formulas are legendary in beaver trapper circles. Old-timers have, after carefully promoting an aura of awe and magic to their lures, induced either jealousy or a reverence among their rivals. While some trappers have carried their secret formulas with them to their graves, others have bequeathed them to heirs or benefactors—after swearing them to secrecy. Some of these sophisticated formulas contained as many as twenty components, and others consisted of as few as three. All were designed to entice the beaver as well as to compete with the lures of fellow trappers. Obviously, these irresistible formulas worked quite well, as evidenced by the beaver population plight a hundred years ago.

With the help of hints from those trappers prospering from their secret formulas I have experimented with lures, creating simple but effective formulas. Usually I mix finely cut beaver castor and beaver oil with a few drops of turpentine or oil of anise added. The oil of anise and turpentine, both plant extracts, represent food components that are rare and exotic to the beaver. Both are pungent and long lasting. I used turpentine and oil of anise alternately—one for two or three years, then the other. Used together, no doubt they would be just as effective— perhaps more so, but I separate them merely for the change of lure.

## The Family in Beaver Society

The beaver family (also called a colony) is the heart of the species' social order. Beginning with the newly-formed pair of two-year-olds, the unit eventually consists of the parents, who mate for life, their yearling offspring (animals in the second year of life) and their young (less than a year old). Just before the mother gives birth to the young, she sends her mate and the yearlings from the lodge and its immediate surroundings. The yearlings usually, but not always, remain in nearby auxilliary ponds, housing themselves in bank dens. The adult male wanders unrestictably about looking for choice food. Allowed to return to the house after a few weeks, he helps with feeding by carrying twigs to the young. The yearlings however, are not welcome at the lodge until near food storage time in the fall. Then, all but the youngest pitch in to make a common provision for winter. They build up and tighten the dams, reshingle the roof of the house with a new coat of mud, dig canals and tunnels, and prepare a cache of food. The family spends the winter together harmoniously, but as soon as the weather warms up following the ice break, the young beavers approaching two years of age move out to make room again for the soon-expected young, in addition to starting their own adult lives. Thus, for about a month prior to the birth of the new generation, the family unit consists of only the parents and the near-yearling litter of the previous year.

## Territorial Behavior

Territorial behavior, or territoriality, in the animal kingdom is denfined as the act of claiming and defending a certain well-defined area. We humans might liken it to staking a mining claim and physically defending it against encroachment by other men. In the world of nature, it is the act of defending a certain area against trespass by other members of the same species, and more particularly, by the same sex of the same species. Sometimes all visitors, as well as intruders of other species are excluded.* For example, who among us would venture near the mother bear or the cow moose when their offspring are very young? Most mammals practice territoriality, especially during reproductive seasons.

Territorial behavior differs among the various species in time, intensity, size of territory, and sex of the defenders. A defended territory might remain stationary, as with a nesting bird; move occasionally, as with a predator moving its young as the grazing food supply moves; or it might move constantly, as with a bull elk defending his grazing harem during the rut.

The duration in time of territorial defense varies from momentary to the entire mature life span of the defendant. For example, in breeding season the sage grouse fly to their lek grounds at daybreak, where the males each claim a few square yards of land and attempt to attract females to their newly-acquired territory while excluding other males from it. After only a few hours the party breaks up, disperses to various feeding grounds, and then roosts until the following morning when they repeat the performance of the preceding day, each with a new territory but in the same area. Robin's and hornet's nests represent seasonal territoriality during the mating and rearing

---

* Once a pair of duck hawks nested near the horse trail where I had occasion to ride quite frequently. On my first few trips they warned me with their typical cries, then buzzed very closely around my head at a terrific speed. Having observed territorial behavior in many species, I was quite amused, concluding their actions to be brave bluff. But finally, one contacted my bald head with bulletlike speed, drawing blood—even though I was wearing my hat. I hastened my journey!

seasons. A year-round, or permanent territorial behavior, is well exemplified by the beaver, though it also exhibits seasons of greater and less intensity of territorial behavior. Territorial behavior in beaver is more intense during spring and summer, and less so in fall and winter.

Of what consequence is territorial behavior to the welfare of the species involved? After mating and nesting, territoriality ranks next in importance, and in all cases stands crucial to the survival of the species. A territory claimed by a pair of animals denotes a family unit. It provides for a home sanctuary, space to provide a food supply, and protection for the young. It also aids in geographical distribution of the species by causing the individuals to space themselves more evenly over their ranges, lessening the hazards of food shortage and communicable disease.

**Territory and Home Range Compared.** The total area in which an animal lives and travels—where it hunts its food, sleeps, rears its young—marks the home range. Should an animal attempt to exclude all others of its species, except its mate and young offspring, from this entire area, then its home range and its territory are synonymous. But if the animal defends only a part of its home range, such as its den or nest site, against trespass by others of its species, its territory then consists of that specific portion of its home range. Home ranges can, and often do,

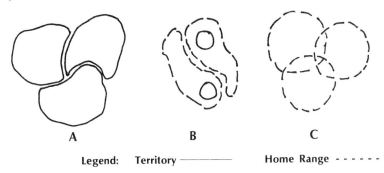

Legend:   Territory ————   Home Range - - - - - -

A comparison of territory and home range. A. where entire home range is defended as territory, there is no overlap. B. most territory is defended as a nest or den site and its close vicinity, small portions of the home range. C. home ranges can and often do overlap.

overlap—an indication that parts of them are shared. Territory, however, is not willingly shared, so they do not overlap. When territorial conflicts arise, the dominant contender enlarges its territory at the expense of the subordinate—representing survival of the fittest.

**Territorial Behavior in Beavers.** The adult sow (female) beaver takes command, not only of her household, but also of a certain area around the house and up and down the stream or shore. The extent of her holdings depend not only on her age, size and physical strength, but also on the time of year and the size of the pond or stream.

It is well known among fur trappers that more beavers inhabit large streams over small ones, even where food plants abound along the small feeder streams. However, on a creek about 50 feet (17 meters) across—not a very large one—I once captured two pregnant beavers at the same location only two nights apart, which is very unusual. This would never happen on a smaller feeder stream, as beavers typically refuse to live that close together.

Though beavers claim as territory, both banks of small streams, they usually claim territory only along one bank of larger streams. Where beavers claim only one bank, estimates of both stream widths and the distance from the banks to the center of the pond or stream have not been made. Undoubtedly, such distances would vary according to the nature of individual beavers, just as the claim of territorial waters of different countries vary.

The adult sow (the matriarch) prohibits any strange beaver to tarry, even briefly, in her quarters. And if the trespasser dares to take his time about moving on, the beaver will not hesitate to kill the intruder. On several occasions, I have trapped two-year-old beavers whose entire bodies were severely lacerated. It is highly probable that these were migratory beavers which became trapped, unable to escape the territory of the sow, and thus suffered the consequences.

The territorial mood of the sow beaver varies considerably with the seasons. During the fall and winter she becomes more tolerant, probably because the young need less care and protection. Hence, she permits all family members, including last year's litter, to assemble at the lodge to spend the winter.

The boar (adult male) beaver plays a secondary and subordinate role in the defense of the family territory, evidenced by the long trips he may take away from home. He may get "up tight" if another adult male comes around, and fight for what is his, but a strange female trespassing his claim does not rouse his anger as easily. In fact, he may become a bit nosey, and even dabble at polygamy if his wife were not so protective and overseeing.

Perhaps the male beaver has been misjudged. It could easily be that a division of responsibility causes territorial behavioral differences between the sexes. It could be that the female is responsible for ruling near the home and the male defending the outposts, being that the rationale for the territorial behaviors among beavers has yet to be completely justified. These are questions for which we just don't have answers yet.

After the ice breaks and the water rises the beavers drawing near two years of age leave the entire home range. Then as the time approaches for the new litter of young to arrive, the boar and the yearlings must also leave the lodge, but are permitted to remain within the home range boundaries. Most of them do remain near, but occasionally a yearling will drift so far from home that its return might be doubtful. The boar might also wander some distance—up to a mile from my observations, and perhaps much farther—but he will return to the lodge after the young are a few days or weeks old.

## The Plight and Adventures of Two-Year Old Beavers

The commencement of the spring water runoff and the rising of the streams signalizes beaver migration—the movement of the two-year-olds to find mates and to establish home ranges of their own. It remains unknown whether the parent beavers disown this group and force them to leave home or whether they develop the urge to find mates and therefore leave voluntarily. The former probably pulls more weight since maturation and sexual development produce a glandular substance which causes the two-year-olds to smell like mature beavers, qualifying them for mating. Amazingly, this new odor, estranges them from their parents, who perhaps construe them as challengers—a threat to the family domain.

The exodus of the two-year-old beavers from their home ranges creates a "floating" beaver population in addition to the resident population. How far they will wander depends largely upon the beaver population level in the area. If the beaver population is low, finding a mate could be more of a problem than finding suitable unclaimed sites for residence. On the other hand, should there exist a large population of beavers, the transient beavers face resistance and often attack while searching for a home site of their own. Evidence reveals that numbers of them receive severe lacerations on their backs—usually above the hips—during spring migration. These wounds affect the fur trapper as well, for holes in the skin cause the pelt to be sharply downgraded, making it less profitable to trap beavers during springtime after the migration is under way.

While some trappers claim that the springtime movement of two-year-old beavers always runs upstream, this obviously cannot be so, or *all* two-year-olds would soon meet together at the very heads of watersheds. The movement progresses both upstream and downstream, with upstream travel much more noticeable because it requires slow and laborious effort and takes place near the water's edge to avoid the current. Downstream travel, on the other hand, moves very rapidly with the current. Most traveling, like other beaver activities, begins at night soon after sunset. Streams are usually high and muddy during migration, making concealed cover for daytime rest difficult for the traveling beaver to locate, so days are often spent humped beneath a willow bush.

Not all two-year-olds confine their travels to the waterways. Some follow the water to its source, and the more adventuresome proceed over the divide to another drainage. I have seen their tracks in the mud of melting snowdrifts on hydrographic divides far from water. One man reported meeting a beaver face to face on a horse trail on a high mountain divide. This overland pilgrimage is probably before the single beavers have found a mate, and happens in spring or early summer when the weather is damp and cool and the water runoff is profuse. In fact, most two-year-old movement, including pairing, usually occurs during the high water period.

While most beavers travel no farther than necessary to find mates and suitable available habitat, a few journey far. Having conducted several studies on the movement of the beaver, the state game department tagging and retrapping programs indicate that some beavers have actually traveled in excess of a hundred miles (160 km) in a single season. Obviously, population levels and crowding influence the extent of their travels, which is perhaps one reason for the distribution of the species over most of the North American continent.

## Other Floaters

In addition to the two-year-olds, the floating segment of the beaver population also consists of a number of adults who do not have mates. These adults do not exhibit territorial behavior, perhaps because they never belong to a family social structure and remain unwelcome in residential territory. Whether or not an adult transient beaver has ever had a mate and claimed a territory, or whether it has any desire to do so, or whether all beavers of reproductive age eventually remate following the death of a mate, can only be speculated upon. However, judging from the numbers of adult transients, it appears a few beavers never mate and acquire residence. From the preponderance of males in this group, it appears that sows who lose mates are more likely to remate as compared to boars who lose mates. An explanation for this could be that since widowed sows usually continue to claim and defend their homes, they have an urge to repopulate it. On the other hand, widower males seldom remain at home and maintain a territory.

The adult transient beavers are distinquished by their "suntans." Their fur often weathers to an ugly copper cast—most undesirable from a fur marketing standpoint.

Building behavior and territorial behavior are interdependent, family-based, and family dependent. In other words, a part of the family social structure. I have never known a lone beaver to cache food or to build a lodge. They do, however, occasionally build a campsite on a small stream by constructing a few small dams for security while sojourning there. Also, since transients must settle down somewhere for the winter, some of them secure temporary provision, such as a deep pond. As previously indicated, some widowed sows continue to occupy the lodge and main pond, but no longer continue building or food caching, which eliminates time spent on repairs, and they may relinquish some home range.

## Interfamily Relationships

Little is known about communication and interactions between neighboring beaver colonies. Are beaver families acquainted with their closest neighbors? Do they respect their neighbors' property rights? Experiments with foxes and raccoons indicate that these animals recognize their neighbors. But, since all animals migrate in response to changes in their environment, such as climate and food supply, it follows that their home ranges also must change, and thus their neighbors.

Beaver families also move short distances and relocate. The move might be motivated by food or water conditions, the filling of the pond by silt, or the presence of enemies (amateur trappers for example). From my observations, it appears that though beavers prefer virgin territory over that taken by conquest, when population levels are high and pressures for space are great, fighting over territory occurs and established families are sometimes forced to relinquish some territory. The confrontation between families being in too close proximity might vary from a mere boundary dispute to total eviction of a young family lacking sufficient physical power to defend its territorial claim.

It appears, then, that beavers recognize the property rights of their neighbors, especially those whose home ranges come in contact with their's. Since it is easier to ignore and avoid other beavers than to fight, beavers probably honor the property rights of their neighbors as a matter of mutual convenience. But for all practical purposes, the social structure of beavers remains intrafamily, with interfamily relationships only apparent during times of overpopulation.

## Pairing or Mating of Beavers

The sexual behavior of beavers—the nature and degree of selectivity, and the timing involved in the pairing of beavers—raises several questions. For example, since breeding occurs several months after the pair-bond formation, what part does the sex urge play in the selection of mates? Is there active competition by either sex for certain mates? Is a display of courtship behavior involved? Are like sexes antagonistic when they meet? And do siblings (brother and sister) mate, or do they avoid each other?

If nothing more is involved in mate selection than sexual recognition, we might expect a very rapid accomplishment of the pairing process all up and down each stream or lake shore. And this would probably involve some pairing of siblings. But, since pair formation occurs long before breeding, it appears that both sexes discriminately choose their lifelong mates, implying that more than the sexual intercourse drive is involved. Based on our knowledge of both human and other mammalian courtship behavior—which involves some antagonism between individuals of the same sex—it can be surmised that beavers sometimes compete for certain mates. This could account for some of the lacerations inflicted upon the floating beaver population.

The question of siblings mating has been presented to me on a number of occasions. It is entirely possible that a beaver might possess an inhibition against mating its sibling, but the mating of siblings is certainly not a beaver taboo carved in stone. A pair of beavers, placed on an isolated stream, will soon have it populated, indicating that siblings and other close relatives will mate, rather than remain unmated. And, it could be that after a period of separation, siblings no longer recognize each other as such. In other words, after wandering for a few weeks or months they might forget what their brothers and sisters smelled like.

The pairing process peaks during the spring water runoff—which varies according to latitude and altitude—then gradually phases out as the summer progresses and the remaining unsuccessful two-year-olds seek mates. Actual pairing dates or occurrences, are not obtainable as the first indication of a new pair of beavers is the construction of a home site in mid- to late-summer. However, on June 11, 1965, I discovered two beavers recently killed by traffic on a streamside highway. The two-year-old beavers, of opposite sex, lying six to eight feet apart, were probably a new pair in quest of a home site.

**Copulation.** According to Mark Weaver, probably the foremost authority in breeding beavers in captivity, copulation of the sexes only occurs in water, and requires a water depth of at least one foot (.3 m). The sow floats on her back and the male rides on top, engaging face to face (ventral sides). The male places his arms about the body of the female to hold himself in place. Weaver found that a front foot or leg impairment or injury prevents the male from staying in place during copulation, which disqualifies him from breeding. Since most beavers breed during the freeze-up of January or February copulation takes place in the tunnel-way near the lodge entrance.

**Desertion?** The preponderance of transient, and apparently unmated, adult males over females during springtime suggests the possibility of desertion by the male. This is pure speculation, however, and further study might reveal that some males either desert their mates or remain faithful but go far from home, perhaps exploring for new and more promising habitat on which to resettle their families. The resolution of these suppositions awaits further study.

## Beaver Play

Though no one has ever accused the beaver of being anything but business-like, considerable play activity ensues within the family; particularly "tag" and frolic.

## Chapter Seven

# BEAVER COMMUNITY & BIOTIC SUCCESSION

An ecological community is customarily named in honor of its dominant primary producer—the major plant growing there. Thus, we are taking liberties with tradition in bestowing such a recognition to the beaver—an animal, and also one but few in number. There are certain areas, however, in which the beaver plays such a dominant role in ecosystem development and maintenance that he is actually the mainstay of those local ecosystems in which he resides. Such areas are along the small feeder streams wherein the works of the beaver have made possible the residence of fishes, toads, frogs, ducks—to name but a few of the water-loving creatures—both plant and animal—which otherwise would not be able to live along such small streams.

Though there are often more beavers along large bodies of water, their impact on the environment is minimal. Thus they do not qualify as dominant species there, and do not deserve comunity recognition.

While the average big-water beaver might make a normal contribution to the community in which he lives—be it a willow community or a cottonwood community, but not a beaver community—his activities will not extend beyond reproduction, consuming vegetable matter, and consigning his waste products to the decomposers for recycling. Eventually, he might become food for a carnivore or yield his pelage (fur) to the use of man.

Our designation of beaver community exists only where there are *beaver dams*. Thus, the beaver gains community dominance only through his engineering excellence, that is engineering development sufficient to alter the habitat and effect a change in the makeup of the kinds of plants and animals which live there. It remains a beaver community only so long as beavers remain there to sustain it.

Before a beaver community is built certain habitat criteria must exist. For example, along the small feeder streams, there is usually an adequate food supply—willows and/or poplars—but not sufficient water to assure substantial safety for the land-awkward beaver. When a pair of exploring beavers discover unclaimed territory on such a stream, they create the needed water environment by impounding the stream. The pond forms the nucleus of what may someday be a beaver community.

Beaver communities might be built in a closely-linked series along a stream, at occasional intervals, or in isolated locations such as on a small spring surrounded by desert-like terrain. The locations depend upon availability of resources which will sustain beavers.

## The Pioneer Phase of Biotic Succession

In addition to the beaver's relatives—the muskrats and the voles—nearby plants and animals which thrive better in a moist or water habitat move in and share the beaver's newly-made home. Even though these first animal visitors—explorers of the water way—may already reside in small numbers along the stream and are tempted to seek both the protection and pleasure offered by the pond, they cannot take up residence or even stay long on the first visit, because there is not yet an adequate food supply for them. Indeed, this pioneer community offers its citizens very little except hard work. The beavers, themselves, are often forced to move away, for though beavers thrive on hard work, they must also have food and building materials, the supply of which they might well deplete in a few years.

Once a family of beavers is forced to abandon its pioneer

**The first pioneers establish a small pond and a bank den. Note the trees standing in the pond. The water will kill them within months.**

home and ponds many years may pass before sufficient vegetation grows to attract another pair of pioneers to that location. The general beaver population, or the demand for new home sites also affect the timing. In the meantime abandoned dams and lodges will fall into disrepair, leak, then rot away within a few years. All that remains is the bit of new soil added from the silt trapped by the dams and the rotted building materials. But the new soil supports a few more plants, perhaps even one or more new species, and succession humbly commences.

Beavers eventually return to the abandoned pioneer site and build anew, their efforts almost as trying and vain as those of their predeccessors. But the struggles of each succeeding settlement of beavers adds new depth and fertility to the soil, which harbors microorganisms—bacteria, protoza—and numerous larger invertebrates—bugs and worms—the pillars in every biological community. The deeper and richer the soil becomes, the more bugs and worms it can harbor and feed, they being in turn food for larger animals. The increase of humus, provided by the increased number of dying plant stalks, adds to the soil's water-holding capacity, enhancing still more vegetative growth. As the soil builds up, the stream bottom becomes broader providing more area for hydric (moist habitat) plants, such as willows. Willows, perhaps one of the most important organisms, flourish, as biotic succession continues toward a functional beaver community. Willows not only provide food and building material for beavers, but home sites and cover for a number of birds and small mammals. Their abundance ultimately aids in more permanently settling the beaver, thus ending the pioneer phase of succession.

## The Intermediate Phase

The dominance of willows characterizes the intermediate phase of biotic succession in the beaver community. For this reason, most biologists would designate it a willow community. Willows grow up through the beaver dams, both the present dam and former dams. Often there will be willows growing in variously shaped lines some distance from the stream. These are the sites of former beaver dams, indicating that there have been changes or shifts in the location of the stream channel. These changes sometimes occur during spring runoff when the excess water current is diverted by beaver dams, washing new channels across stream bends or into former partially silt-filled channels. The beavers wait until late summer then rebuild above the riffles in the stream.

Thus, relative permanence of beaver settlement in an area doesn't mean that each dam and lodge is permanently located. There is a frequent shift in the center of activity and relocation of headquarters as the stream channel shifts, silt fills ponds and as food supply regrows in one locality while being depleted in another. The result is a long term remarkably uniform overall build up of the stream bottomland.

It appears reasonable to believe that the ultimate has now been reached—that almost ever-present beavers should keep conditions quite uniform. Such is not the case, however, for grasses and sedges are also present in this enviroment. They prove to be formidable competitors to the willows. The conditions permitting beaver dominance also seals the doom of

A pioneer beaver home site which has been abandoned for 3 to 5 years. Note: The crumbling dam at left with young willows growing in it; the considerable mud and silt deposits just behind the dam and on either side of the present stream channel; the vegetation beginning to grow in the silt deposits; and the devastation of the old aspen growth, and new aspen growth in the foreground.

An early springtime view of the intermediate stage.

Late beaver stage. Note the section of dam (right of center) in which sedges have replaced willows as part of the dam. The lodge in the distance (see arrow) is constructed largely of mud and small willow sticks.

In this view of the late beaver stage, the willows are almost depleted, the beaver lodge (arrow) is constructed with a large proportion of mud, and the length of the pond is greatly reduced by mud and sedges.

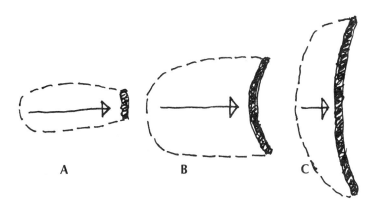

Diagram of dam-pond size and shape relationships as succession proceeds. A. typical pioneer stage with short dam and long, narrow pond. B. typical intermediate stage as bottomland broadens and prior to serious silting. C. typical terminal stage with long dam and pond filled with silt except where beavers have kept it dredged.

the beaver community. Its decline begins when the grasses and sedges become dominant over the willows. As the willows become less plentiful, beavers overgraze them and further hasten their disappearance.

Typical beaver pond shapes change as biotic succession progresses. This results from the broadening of the bottomland and the shift in dominance from willows to grasses and sedges.

Changes in the makeup of the animal life coincide with the changes in plants and pond characteristics. It should be noted that the greatest diversity of life occurs during the intermediate phase: There is not only more water, but also a greater variety of shrubs (willows), sedges, and grasses, than during other stages. In short, more food and cover for more kinds of life prevails during this phase. The transition toward meadow during the intermediate phase happens so slowly that the beaver community remains quite stable. (Some differences between the biotic makeup of a beaver community and a nearby habitat without beavers is summarized on page 92.)

## Comparison of a Beaver Habitat
## and a No-beaver Habitat

**About 2 kilometers (1.2 mi.) apart on the same stream.**

| BEAVER HABITAT | NO-BEAVER HABITAT |
|---|---|
| **Flora** | **Flora** |
| sedges *(Carex spp.)* | bluegrass *(Poa pratensis)* |
| redtop *(Agrostis alba)* | Idaho fescue *(Festica idahoenssi)* |
| white clover *(Trifolium repens)* | sagebrush *(Artemisia* spp.) |
| willows *(Salix* spp.) | willows *(Salix* spp.) |
| **Fauna** | **Fauna** |
| robin *(Turdus migratorius)* | robin *(Turdus migratorius)* |
| meadowlark *(Sturnella neglecta)* | meadowlark *(S. neglecta)* |
| black-billed magpie *(Pica pica)* | black-billed magpie *(P. pica)* |
| sandhill crane *(Grus canadensis)* | sage sparrow *(Amphispiza belli)* |
| blue heron *(Ardea herodias)* | |
| mallard duck *(Anas platyrhynchos)* | |
| meadow vole *(Microtus pennsylvanicus)* | meadow vole *(M. pennsylvanicus)* |
| water vole *(M. pennsylvanicus macropus)* | western jumping mouse *(Zapa princeps)* |
| muskrat *(Ondatra zibethicus)* | pocket gopher *(Thomomys bottae)* |
| moose *(Alces alces)* | |
| water snake *(Natrix sipedon)* | |
| tiger salamander *(Ambystoma tigrinum)* | |
| cutthroat trout *(Salmo clarki)* | |

**Beavers & Other Species.** Few scientific experiments have been conducted to measure the interaction of beavers with the other species that enjoy the use of their ponds. Since beavers are strict vegetarians, and not a popular or easily accessible prey species due to their protective home environment, their association with other mammals is largely confined to their relatives, the muskrats, and the meadow and water voles. Still, even though these animals share the pond and compete with the beaver in a very minor way for the abundance of grasses and roots, he apparently pays little or no attention to them. Ecologically, the animal residents in the beaver community are commensals to the beaver. That is, they depend upon him for their habitat. It might be fairly accurate to say that the secondary consumers are commensal to the beaver, but the beaver is commensal to the food plants in its community.

The ecological relationship of beaver and trout has long been a subject of varying opinions. From the results of studies made under quite different conditions, it would appear that the beaver's effects upon fishing varies widely from place to place and from time to time, and depends upon such conditions as altitude, trout species, trout spawning habits, terrain, water temperature, stream swiftness, and plant life in the area.

In Michigan, studies concluded that beavers distressed trout habitat in slow-moving streams by causing unfavorable ecological changes. For example, new life grew rapidly in beaver ponds and competed for the oxygen supply in the water, thus causing oxygen shortages to trout. Silt trapped behind beaver dams covered spawning sites. Fluctuations in water temperature in beaver impoundments interfered with spawning. Climax beaver ponds filled with silt and became meadows. And due to warmer temperature in slow moving ponds, parasites increased in fish, and the fish were less palatable.

Quite different results emerged in Wyoming, where studies indicated a beneficial effect of beavers upon trout. These studies were made high in the mountains where water temperatures remain cool, and at sites where neither beavers nor trout had existed before being planted there by state workers. Trout flourished and fishing was good.

In the beaver community few, if any, trout existed there

before the beaver. Therefore, if there are no trout in a particular beaver community, the beaver has done them no harm. If there are trout—and there usually are—the beaver is their benefactor, as he has provided the pond in which they live.

The beaver directly interacts with its food plant species, some of which are also used as building material. Somewhat wasteful of the plants at times, the beaver will deplete them and to his own detriment, should the beaver population become too large. The beaver also interrelates with the grasses, but not extensively; they are of minor importance to the beaver's diet.

The beaver hosts two ectoparasites—lice and fleas. Though these parasites have very little direct effect upon their hosts, partly because comparatively few beavers get them, the bugs can transmit the beaver's most devasting disease organism, *Bacterium tularense*, the causative agent of tularemia—a beaver killer.

**Beaver Abandonment—Community Effects.** Because the beaver is neither numerous nor an important prey species, a rapid beaver population decline to a near-zero level has little effect upon nature's balance outside the beaver community. Within the beaver community, however, the effects are quite different, with the late pioneer and intermediate communities suffering the most loss. As the dams wash out and the ponds dry, the affected species either migrate or die off. The nearer the community approaches beaver climax, the less dependent it is upon the beaver's actual presence because the dams have become more permanent and the meadows more capable of self sustenance (see Climax and Decline).

**Food Chain.** The line of food acquisition ascending up the trophic levels of the food pyramid is referred to as the food chain. An incident I once observed exemplifies the food chain in the beaver community. In a small canyon heavily forested by spruce, with a few willows and aspen, some beavers had established a pioneer community near the head of the water. They built a large dam and a large house, and depleted the aspens and willows after a few years, then moved away. The following spring a pair of sandhill cranes nested atop the house (they, too, like the protection of water on all sides). After hatching their brood, they moved out to the lush grass at the head of the pond near the spruce trees. When I happened by, I flushed the parent cranes who came honking wildly just over my head. After spending a few seconds of enchantment at their closeness and majesty, I turned to see a peregrine falcon trying to lift something from the ground. Upon scaring the hawk away, I discovered a dying sandhill crane chick.

Sandhill cranes normally lay two eggs; I found only one chick. Perhaps the hawk had already killed the other one. The hawks built their nest in a tall spruce near the pond. They too, had a family to feed. While not hunting afield, they perched above the pond and silently watched and awaited their opportunity.

Such incidents depict the essential constitution of life on earth—the balancing of nature and the economical regulation of a community of life. In this case, the beavers provided the habitat for the cranes—plenty of grass and an ideal nesting site. Whether the beavers' presence influenced the hawks in their selection of a nesting site is doubtful. It is probable that they were there because of other favorable features of the habitat and, of course, the availability of the territory, for they, too, have a system of distribution based on territorial behavior.

Many variations of the above example could be discovered in beaver communities. The species involved might vary widely, but the food chain pattern is always the same—the primary consumers (herbivores) feed upon the producers (green plants), the secondary consumers (carnivores) feed upon the primary consumers, and in many cases, these are fed upon by tertiary consumers.

**Water & Soil Conservation.** Research on the need to conserve soil and water strongly implies that soil erosion and water depletion are caused by the careless and greedy acts of some people. This is at least partly true, but further examination offers a broader perspective.

The earth's crust, in constant motion, has caused the formation of continents, mountains and deep seas. Except when a volcano erupts or there is a major earthquake, the slow movement of the earth's crust cannot be perceived by humans. Other forces work at leveling the upheavels caused by the movement of the earth's crust. For example, water and weather constantly chip away at the land mass and gravity acts upon both the particles and water, carrying land debris back into the seas. It has been estimated that the Mississippi River carries and deposits into the Gulf of Mexico from two to three million tons of solids every day, lengthening the delta about 120 feet (40 meters) each year. Thus, two counteracting forces cycle the materials in the earth's crust. Were it not for a third force, which greatly impedes this erosive process, the seas might be filled much more rapidly than the crust is heaved up. The terrestrial plant life accounts for most of this impediment. Their roots anchor the soil, and the humus, formed from dead leaves and stalks, makes a sponge which holds rain and snow water, permitting it time to permeate the deeper soil. This nourishes the plant life and also slows the seaward onrush of water carrying solids. The more prolific the plant life, the slower the erosion of the earth, and vice versa.

The beaver is another natural agent whose activities along small streams aid in the conservation of water, flood control and the arrest of soil erosion, all which greatly contribute to the welfare of man and nature.

**Water Storage in Beaver Impoundments.** Grasse & Putnam (1955) measured the water stored in one very large beaver pond in Wyoming and calculated it to be more than ten million cubic feet, or more than 75 million gallons! They also measured the stream's inflow to the pond and calculated that should it cease entirely, there would be enough water in the pond for an outflow, at the same rate, for 117 days! This was an exceptional pond to be sure. Reason tells us that a number of smaller impoundments would store a similar amount of water as well. Grasse and Putnam also noted that another stream flowed twice as abundantly a quarter mile below its beaver impoundments than it did immediately below them, indicating seepage of water through the soil from the impoundments.

In a limited study on the water content of soils in beaver ecosystems, I compared soil between a series of beaver ponds with soil about a mile (approx 1.7 kilometers) down the same small stream where there were no beavers and where perhaps none had ever resided. The soil, about fifty feet (approx. 16 meters) from stream center between beaver dams, contained an average of 48.7% water. Soil the same distance from center where there were no beaver ponds contained an average of 24.5% water—or about half as much. Even though the water content of soil varies widely among different soils and according to the season, the test indicates that the soil in that particular beaver ecosystem contained approximately 31 pounds of water per cubic foot, which equals about 151,000 gallons per acre-foot. Thus, more than 75,000 gallons more water was stored in an acre-foot of soil in the beaver ecosystem than in the soil on the same stream where there were no beavers.

A water environment is essential to all life. Some forms are adapted to more of it, some to less. The shortage of water on land limits the abundance of life to be found there—both numbers of species and individuals within species. Thus, water flow regulation and conservation enriches the earth, increases its carrying capacity of living creatures and enlarges the food web.

**Soil Conservation in Beaver Impoundments.** Beaver ponds serve as sedimentation reservoirs by (1) slowing the stream current and thus allowing particles more dense than water to settle out, and (2) trapping the less dense particles in the upper dam structure as the water filters through it. In an experiment to illustrate this, water samples were taken above and below a series of ten various-sized dams on a small stream where the beaver community succession was near climax. The dams varied in width from about 50 to 200 feet (15.4 to 61 meters, approx.). The drainage above the dams was small—perhaps four square miles— and heavily timbered on the north slopes, with mixed shrubery and aspens on the south slopes. The samples, taken on June 6th, as the spring runoff and silt content were beginning to recede, were filtered, oven dried, and the solid matter was weighed on analytical balances. The water above the dams carried 0.1089 grams of solids per liter. The water below the dams carried 0.0407 grams per liter. Left as sediment behind the dams was 0.0682 grams per liter, or 62.64 percent of the solids carried by the water.

In converting these data into the English system and expanding them to more useful proportions, the rate of sedimentation stands at approximately 185 pounds per acre foot of water flowing through the system of dams. This does not tell us all, of course. The rate of sedimentation per day or per year could be determined by measuring the stream flow and the length of time it takes to move through the beaver dam system—an interesting study to anticipate.

## Climax And Decline

Ironically, it is sometimes the very elements of success which bring about the decline and end to an era. The decline of the beaver community comes about so slowly as to be almost imperceptible. But, a careful observer can discern the various stages of the process. Although the beaver can eat almost any vegetation and can build with almost any material, he will not long remain in a habitat devoid of palatable woody plants. Curtailment in the use of wood products and a corresponding increase in the use of mud in the construction of dams and lodges then, signifies a decline of beaver dominance in a community. As the dams become more earthen, and thus more permanent, they become more suitable habitat for willows—then for grasses. The earth also harbors decomposers, organisms which hasten the decay and recycling of the wood components and the transition from wooden to earthen dams. The same transition takes place in the lodges, though sufficient wood must be used for a supporting framework. The climax and post climax lodge is very dark in color, appearing more as an earthen mound, whereas the lodge in the pioneer community appears as a wooden house. In the succession toward climax, the wood-to-earth ratio of beaver structures corresponds closely to the stage of succession.

Simultaneous with the transition taking place in the dams and lodges is the silting, and consequent shrinking, of the ponds. The beaver, a master excavator, continually builds up by dredging from the pond bottom and building atop the dams. The dredging occurs mostly near the dam, however, and the pond shrinks from the far end. As the silt continues to build up, aquatic sedges invade the shallows and the decomposers soon begin adding the dead annual stalks of sedges to the fill.

The beaver at last engages in a literal "last ditch stand" to preserve his habitat. He succeeds only so long as sufficient woody plants remain to sustain his needs.

The beaver community thus falls, not by default or by negligence of its founder and leading citizen, but by the very Utopian condition he created. The community makeup has changed during this long decline of beaver prominence, but very slowly. The aquatic forms have given way to those preferring merely a moist habitat, but the area's worth to man has not diminished—and what a delightful contrast to the semi-barren state it was before Mr. and Mrs. Beaver arrived the first time!

An abandoned site, at the late willow-beaver stage. Note that the dam has been cut at the far end and that the willows are much depleted. Sedges have invaded much of the pond.

## Chapter Eight

# MANAGEMENT OF THE BEAVER RESOURCE

Questions concerning the ethics of beaver trapping are raised time and time again. It is often asked if the beaver should not simply be left alone and allow Nature to regulate its population levels. However, not only hunters themselves, but even the most ecologically-minded individuals entertain the concept that it is much more humane to control population levels by man than by starvation and disease.

## Why Manage the Beaver?

All species reproduce so prolifically that without limiting circumstances their populations would increase boundlessly—fill the whole earth. But actually, in the long term, the numbers of individuals in a given species tend to remain about the same, though with wide short term fluctuations—and in balance with the rest of nature's creatures. The excess individuals produced each generation must be able to acquire protection and life's necessities or perish. Thus, when a population increases to the extent that it is short of food, space or water; or disease breaks out (limiting factors to population abundance), some individuals must die. Predators slow this process by taking some of the increase in prey animals.

The population of the beaver, a prey animal, is naturally

stabilized by these same limiting factors. When too many beavers are looking for food and a place to live, they consume the available food supply, and they fight for space (territory), including open water. If many do not die from these conditions, communicable disease intervenes, causing a rapid and severe die-off in the population.

Migrating two-year-old beavers, not having established protective structures, are most vulnerable to predation. They are also the segment of the population which spreads tularemia, a disease capable of reducing a local population to near zero. Tularemia, caused by *Bacterium tularense*, often strikes wild animal populations, especially the rodents such as mice, rabbits, muskrats and beavers. Biting ectoparasites (external parasites) such as ticks, lice and fleas, are the vectors which spread tularemia from host to host. Thus a beaver in transit may transmit the bug to other beavers he encounters.

Managing the beaver resource (1) protects the beaver habitat, (2) protects the habitat of the creatures which live among the beavers, and (3) protects the beavers from the "feast and famine" population variations that unmanaged beaver populations suffer.

## Methods

Several methods are available to wildlife conservationists to manage beaver populations, each containing both strong and weak points. A basic understanding of the various methods will aid trappers to choose the appropriate method—the method that will provide optimum sustainable returns.

Managing to keep the beaver population in balance with the beaver's habitat requirements will permit optimum sustainable returns. Should a colony's food supply be threatened by too many beavers *most* should be removed to permit revegetation. On the other hand, should good beaver habitat be under-populated, beavers should not be trapped there, allowing full utilization of the habitat.

Maintaining the beaver population at the level at which it will utilize most of its resources of food, water, space, but not *over*-utilize them, will permit the *optimum* or highest permanent beaver population, and thus, the greatest possible annual harvest.

**The Removal of Two-Year-Olds.** The trapping of transient two-year-old beavers must be done on unclaimed territory to avoid capturing the resident beavers, and thus maintaining the family units. The two-year-old has a fair-sized pelt, making it rather profitable to trap for. In addition, this curious—or investigative—and not yet trap-shy beaver is an easy target. Removing these travelers stops the movement of beaver into areas where they are not wanted.

On the other hand, there are drawbacks to stabilizing the population through trapping the two-year-olds. For one, the trapping season is short—only a few weeks in spring. Fur damage from fighting is more prevalent among the two-year-olds, and pelt size, though fair, is not as large as the market prefers. In the meantime, the untrapped breeding population grows older and eventually will cease reproducing. Thus, in time, the breeding population will be composed of a large number of retirees and production will decrease. Therefore, this method of harvest is not justifiable as a long-term policy for optimum sustainable yield.

**Indiscriminate Trapping.** Indiscriminate trapping, based upon the estimated annual increase of an entire area, simply involves setting traps randomly and taking what comes until the desired number of beavers has been removed. Obviously this "lazy trapper" method of beaver population control—an easy and effective one provided the estimate of increase holds some degree of accuracy—will accomplish a sustainable yield at some level—though lower than optimum, because it leaves many unpaired adults which may never mate again. It is not likely, however, to take into account such problems as food supply trend or production potential in all segments of the area. Some state game departments issue designated areas to individual trappers and merely impose a specified maximum annual trapping quota, or they may have a general season and sell a specified number of beaver pelt tags.

The ecological results of this method appear to be spotty at best.

**Selective Trapping.** Selective trapping is based on individual beaver family analysis. Beaver family analysis is possible only where each family builds a lodge or leaves other evidence of a family unit, usually on small streams and along lake shores. In this option each colony is analyzed to determine which area appears be be underpopulated and which colony should be removed to protect the habitat.

Beavers reach an age at which they cease to reproduce, but continue to religiously exercise dominion over their estates. These are the beavers which should receive first priority in a culling program. They wear the largest and highest valued skins (unusual in live-animal culls), they are consuming (though lightly) but not producing, and they deny the use of their territory to the potential producers. Continued delay in their removal hazards a double loss, for when they die of old age—which they will eventually do—their pelts will be lost.

These "old folks" are easily located along small streams, where family units are easy to spot. On some lakes and rivers it is most difficult to distinguish each family unit when the beaver population is dense and their territory is not as large nor as accurately defined as on a small stream. However, any beaver house in disrepair should be suspect. Close examination of the surroundings will often reveal a slight sign of life. Such places often yield only a single beaver, the mate having died or been trapped.

Desirable as this method of population management is, it can be applied only in a limited way because of the difficulty of analysis in many locations, and some might object to the excessive labor involved. It might be added also, that the elderly beavers are often trap-shy, and thus difficult to capture.

**Periodic Severe Trapping.** This kind of trapping includes elements of the other methods, and is usually the best if done carefully. It involves heavy trapping of an area each time the population approaches a limit—food supply, territory, and/or communicable disease potential (an ever-present intangible which increases rapidly as population increases). Depending upon the severity of the previous trapping, the general beaver population of the region, and the limiting factor(s) involved, trapping of this nature should take place at intervals of three to four years.

Ideally, a trapper removes all beavers except the young and perhaps a few young pairs. If the trapper spends time and effort to exclude young beavers from the catch, only a few adults will escape and few cubs or yearlings will be taken by accident. This management system keeps the breeding herd young, healthy, and vigorous. It also provides for a brief period of replenishment of the food supply. Spread of any prevalent communicable disease is arrested because most communication discontinues for a time. Beaver community life (other species living there) is not disrupted as much as one would suspect, because much of the habitat remains intact. Though minor competitors, such as muskrats, take over vacant houses and ponds, they pose no obstacle to the new beaver generation.

**Rotational Trapping.** Some beaver managers divide a region into management areas, of about the size which one trapper can handle. The trapper then removes all beavers from one fourth of his area each year. This fourth then has a chance to revegitate while it is being repopulated by young immigrant beavers from the other three segments of the area and other places. Thus each area quarter is cleared of beavers very fourth year and has three years in which to repopulate. This method alievates the problem of sexual imbalance and consequent nonbreeders which often results from indiscriminate trapping, where one of a pair may be taken and the other left.

**Live Trapping and Translocation.** Live trapping and then relocating beavers was employed by the various states to reintroduce beavers to the regions from which they had been extirpated.

This method of management has proved effective in many instances. For example, after study on a very small stream in Wyoming indicated that there were no beavers there, nor was there any indication that there had ever been, Grasse & Putnam (1955) planted ten beavers which they had moved from an area of overproduction. One year later, ." . . fifty-five beaver dams, extending in an almost continuous string from the head of the stream for two and one-fourth miles. . . The result was a surprising amount of beaver work done on one stream by ten beaver."

Where populations are maintained at a level consistent with

sound soil and water conservation practices, however, there will still be summertime damage by beavers in some localities. The only alternative to live-trapping and transplanting the offenders is to destroy them while their pelts are worthless.

Beavers released in areas where there are no other beavers should be sexed and released in pairs of similar size and/or age to maximize the probability of compatibility, mating and reproduction.

Obviously, beavers should not be live-trapped and translocated to areas already populated with beavers. And *most* beaver habitat is now occupied.

## Conflict of Interest Between Beaver & Man

For many years the beaver's range has been continuously constricted by the agricultural interests of man. Now it is being further shrunken by the development of roads and campgrounds on public lands. But beavers either fail to understand or refuse to accept the boundaries man has set for their domain. Some of them leave their reservations to plunder or vandalize the works of man: They dam off his irrigation canals, flood his fields and meadows, dine on his fruit and shade trees, stop culverts and flood forest access roads. Too often a *general* population reduction program is then implemented, to the detriment of both beaver and man.

Beaver damage on public lands is tolerated more or less good naturedly by most of the public. Private property damage, however, is something else. The beaver cannot be permitted to infringe upon the legitimate private property rights nor the food production of man. Thus, maintaining a large beaver population on or near some privately owned land becomes difficult. In many instances, for example, private land owners hold grazing rights to the public lands near their deeded property. If the beavers have been a nuisance or damaging to him on his private land, he is prone to develop a bias against all beavers, to view each pond on the public land as an encroachment upon his range rights and a potential threat to his fields nearby.

One of the extremist opposing points of view, however, is that since the public lands belong to the public and the rancher is using them, he is a feeder at the public trough. He has grown rich

Beavers damming bridge sites and flooding roads must be removed.

and fat from his use of land on which he does not even pay the taxes. The wildlife residing on his property do him negligible damage. He should be grateful for the privilege of feeding a few game animals, rodents, and predators.

As in all game management, justice must prevail in beaver management as well. We cannot rightfully expect a few individuals to tolerate the beaver's damaging activities, nor can we permit them to dictate public policy for selfish purposes. If the beaver resource is to be managed for the benefit of mankind, individual man must be protected from the depredations of individual beavers. The management must be even handed and fair to both public and private interests. It must not be left to the emotionalism of either end of the opinion spectrum. In the long run, the conflict between public and private interests is a "tight rope" which policy makers and their administrators must continue to tread.

## Table I
## System for Size Determination of Beaver Pelts

Over 69 inches: super blanket
65 inches to 69 inches: blanket
60 inches to 64 inches: extra large
55 inches to 59 inches: large
50 inches to 54 inches: medium
45 inches to 49 inches: small
Under 45 inches: cub or kitten

Pelt sizes for fur grading purposes are determined from measuring the combined length and width of the pelt. For example, a properly prepared pelt measuring 35 inches in length and 35 inches in width is a 70 inch beaver—a "super blanket"—and it would be perfectly round. A more natural shape, however, is somewhat oval or egg-shaped with the greater dimension in length.

## Table 2
## Beaver Age—Size Relationships

| Age | Weight | Pelt Size* | Total Length | Tail Measurement |
| --- | --- | --- | --- | --- |
| 6 months | 17 lbs. | 49 inches | 32 inches | 4 inches X 8 inches |
| 18 months | 30 lbs. | 60 inches | 37 inches | 4¾ X 9 inches |
| 30 months | 36 lbs. | 63 inches | 40 inches | 5¼ X 10½ inches |
| Mature | 51 lbs. | 70 inches | 45 inches | 6¾ X 11½ inches |
| Mature | 60 lbs. | 74 inches | 48 inches | 7¼ X 12 inches |

* Skinned and processed for market. Pelt size in beaver is determined by the combined measurement of length and width.

# References Used

Aleksiuk, M., 1968. Scent Mound Communication, Territoriality. *Journal of Mammalogy*, Volume 49, pages 759-761.

Allred, M. 1980. A re-emphasis on the value of the beaver in natural resource conservation. *Journal of Idaho Academy of Science*, Volume 16, pages 3-10.

_____. The potential use of beaver population behavior in beaver resource management. *Journal of Idaho Academy of Science*, Volume 17, pages 14-24.

Anderson, W.A. 1959. The angel of Hudson's Bay. *Saturday Evening Post*, January, Volume 24, page 24.

Bailey, V. 1927. Beaver habits and experiments in beaver culture. *Tech. Bull. No. 21. USDA.*

Barash, D. P. 1974. Neighbor recognition in two solitary carnivores; the raccoon *(Procyon lotor)* and the red fox *(Vulpes fulva)*. *Science*, Volume 185, pages 794-796.

Bartlett, D. and J. 1974. Nature's aquatic engineers: beaver. *Nat. Geo.*, Volume 145(5), pages 716-732.

Berry, D. 1961. *A Majority of Scoundrels.* New York, Harper & Brothers.

Bradt, G. W. 1947. *Michigan Beaver Management.* Mich. Dept. of Conservation.

Brenner, F. J. 1967. Spatial and energy requirements of beaver. *Ohio Journal of Science.* 67(4) 242-246.

Brosnan, C. J. 1918. *History of the State of Idaho.* New York, Chas Scribner.

Burdon, K. L. 1949. *Textbook of Microbiology.* New York, Chas Scribner.

Burger, C. 1968. *Beaver Skins and Mountain Men.* New York, Dutton.

Burrows, W., J. W. Moulder, R.M. Lewest and R. Murdock. 1965. *Textbook of Microbiology.* Philadelphia, Saunders.

Butler, R. G. and L. Butler. 1979. Toward a functional interpretation of scent marking in the beaver *(Castor canadensis). Behavioral and Neural Biol.,* Vol. 26, pages 442-454.

Chittenden, H.M. 1935. *The American Fur Trade of the Far West.* New York, Press of the Pioneers, Inc.

Cutright, W.J. and T. McKean. 1978. Countercurrent blood vessel arrangement in beaver *(Castor canadensis). Journal of Morphology.* Volume 16 (2), pages 169-176.

Davis, D.E. and F.B. Golley. 1963. *Principles In Mammalogy.* New York, Reinhold.

Driggs, B. W. (H. Forbush and L. Clements eds). 1970 *History of Teton Valley,* Idaho. Rexburg, ID, Arnold Agency.

*Encyclopedia Americana.* 1956. Canada: Industrial Development 5 (12), page 346.

_____. 1969. Fur Industry: History of Fur Trade. 12 (3) page 178.

Gebhardt, L.P. and D.A. Anderson. 1965. *Microbiology.* St. Louis, Mosby.

Grasse, J.E. and E.V. Putnam. 1950. *Beaver management and ecology.* Wyo. Game & Fish Comm. Bull. No. 6.

Hall, E.R. and K.R. Kelson. 1959. *Mammals of North America.* New York, Ronald.

*Idaho Wildlife Review.* 1968: March - April. Boise.

Innis, H.A. 1964. *The Fur Trade in Canada.* New Haven, Yale.

Jorgenson, J.W., M. Novotny, M. Carmack, G.B. Copland and R.S. Wilson. 1978. Chemical scent constituents in the urine of the red fox *(Vulpes vulpes)* Linn. during the winter season. *Science,* Volume 199, pages 796-798.

Krebs, C.J. 1972. *Ecology: The Experimental Analysis of Distribution and Abundance.* New York, Harper & Row.

Odum, E.P. 1971. *Fundamentals of Ecology.* Philadelphia, Saunders.

Ogden, Peter Skene. 1950. *Ogden's Snake Country Journals.* London, Hudson's Bay Company Records Society.

O'Neil, T. 1949. *The Muskrat in the Louisiana Coastal Marshes.* Louisiana Dept. of Wildlife & Fisheries, New Orleans.

Osborne, R. 1921. *Journal of a Trapper.* Boise, ID, Syms, York.

Rue, L.L. III. 1964 *The World of the Beaver.* New York, Lippencott.

_____. 1967. *Pictorial Guide to Mammals of North America.* New York, Crowell.

Salyer, J.C. 1934. Preliminary report on beaver-trout investigations. *Michigan Dept. of Conservation.*

Sanderson, I.T. *Living Mammals of the World.* Garden City, NY, Hanover.

Selkirt, E.E. (ed.) 1971. *Physiology.* Boston, Little Brown.

Sunder, J. E. 1959. *Bill Sublette, Mountain Man.* Norman, OK, U of Okla. Pr.

Svendsen, G.E. 1978. Castor and anal glands of the beaver. *Journal of Mammalogy,* Volume 59, pages 618-620.

Tevis, L. Jr. 1950. Summer behavior of a family of beavers in New York State. *Journal of Mammalogy,* Volume 31, pages 40-65.